WE PRETEND THEY'RE
FIREWORKS

WE PRETEND THEY'RE FIREWORKS

HANNAH LIN KERNAL

NEW DEGREE PRESS

COPYRIGHT © 2019 HANNAH LIN KERNAL

WE PRETEND THEY'RE FIREWORKS

ISBN   978-1-64137-330-2 *Paperback*

          978-1-64137-640-2 *Ebook*

This book is dedicated to my sister, Sarah Lin Kernal.

Thank you for supporting me unwaveringly.

CONTENTS

"I like to remind myself that every other time I thought something wasn't going to end, it ended."

—JOHN GREEN

AUTHOR'S NOTE

———

Dear Reader,

Before I begin, I want to acknowledge some of the people that have helped make the writing of this possible. I honestly wouldn't be anywhere near this accomplishment without the help and support and encouragement of so many awesome people.

Thank you to Baldeep Pabla, an awesome God-brother-in-law and social worker who's taught me more than I could ever have hoped to know about infrastructure and the complexities of how social welfare is addressed in America. Thank you to Brandon Lien, my kind cousin and registered nurse who's taught me about the intricacies of tending to patients with a frame of care.

And a special thank you to Kalani Newman, my best friend who's been incredibly empathetic for countless late night discussions about depression and mental health. Without you, this book may have never been returned to after I initially abandoned it years ago, and I certainly wouldn't be the person who I am today. It is because you have believed in me that I am now achieving one of my biggest life goals.

I started writing *We Pretend They're Fireworks* when I was still in high school, and it has since then evolved into something totally different than I could have imagined it to be. At first, I had abandoned the novel because I had begun to feel like it wasn't serving any true purpose. It didn't have any themes about mental health, and it certainly wasn't explicitly dystopian fiction. I don't think that I was at a point where I could actually write what I have created today. I think I actually had the novel begin with Blue being successful in his initial jump, which would've made the story entirely different.

But, upon my return to the novel, *Fireworks* grew to include dealings with sexual abuse and issues regarding mental health, neither of which I had allowed myself to explore properly until after the project had been abandoned the first time.

My first romantic relationship, when I was 14 and 15 years old, eventually turned into a sexually abusive one. And, as far as I know, my personal battle with depression has always been something to which I've needed to pay great amounts of care and attention. These two great afflictions of my life culminate themselves into the two main characters of the book, putting the two in conversation with each other in a way that I didn't know I could have ever wanted or needed. Now, my great hope is that the addition of my voice, the addition of my characters' voices, will add to a greater discourse of conversation around these two topics.

The title for the novel was inspired by a conversation I'd had with a couple of cousins about hearing gunshots relatively frequently in their neighborhood. How they commonly dealt with the fear, as one might assume, was that they pretended the shots were fireworks being set off.

And I've dealt with different things very similarly. When depression sneaks its awful head into my life, I've had the tendency to tell myself that I was only making a big deal out of nothing and that there wasn't anything to truly be concerned about. I've had the tendency to convince myself that the sexual abuse and assault have been things which were perfectly avoidablem, and that I've been lying to make things seem larger than they truly are. I've since learned that convincing myself that these problems are only false alarms, has done nothing but harm my mental health and my ability to trust myself, especially when it is the worst for me. Just as the "fireworks" are always real gunshots, my emotional reactions and experiences are not just false alarms. There is a problem at the root that deserves attention, and part of that attention is conversation with others.

I hope that the reading material before you is something you enjoy. But, more than that, I hope it is something that makes you think about, and feel more comfortable with, topics which are normally too taboo for discussion.

Thank you,
Hannah Lin Kernal

PROLOGUE

———

Wake up.
School.
Homework.
Sleep.
Wake up.
Start over.

Most people in Pennyworth call it the "chink's" lifestyle. Acquaintances at school would tell me that they wanted to set me up with cute guys at our school, but as soon as anyone mentioned anything about my being part Asian, the romantic interest in me would stop. Not that it matters much anyway. I have the chink's lifestyle. Not that it doesn't matter that they call me a chink, but I just can't bring myself to care about that anymore. That's how

Pennyworth has always been, and when I first spoke up about it, I was shut down.

What else can you expect?

I live the chink's lifestyle. It shouldn't matter anyway. We chinks just have to deal with how well we do in school, right? Go to college, right? Have our parents yell at us to get work done or else we don't eat, right? It's less of that case when your dad was white though. It means your Asian mom is slightly more laid back than most Asian parents and will make it more of the norm to be slightly laid back. Not super laid back, but more relaxed than you'd expect from a completely Asian household.

I guess that goes for lots of other things too. Now my mom is way more lenient on curfew, meaning if I come back 5 minutes after I say I will she won't get THAT mad at me. As long as my grades don't turn into more "Bs" than "A's," everything is all good. I can even have a significant other if I just tell visiting Asian family members that that person is "just a close friend of mine."

The funny thing is, I wasn't always so busy with school. When I was younger, my dad and I would take bike rides around the city. He would take me to the park and teach me some of the martial arts that he remembered from when he was younger. He used to take me to the back of the park, where there was loads of overgrowth and trees, all the time. I saw little balloons back there and asked him who would waste perfectly good balloons.

"Lacey," he started, "I have a feeling those rubbers weren't wasted. Let's just see that kick again, okay honey?"

I still remember the lilt of joviality he had in his voice, how bemused he was at my not yet knowing. Now I know, obviously, that those weren't balloons. And I laugh at the innocence that I had then. It was funny for both of us to realize that I wouldn't know things in quite the same way when I got older. There came a day where I did know, and he was enjoying it then in the same way. Only I have learned to enjoy it in retrospect.

I reacted enthusiastically at his request for me to kick again. With all the pleasure my little heart could muster, I responded "Ooooo-KAY!" and kicked out as hard as I possibly could on the second syllable, the first one acting as a sort of wind up time. My little five or six or seven year old foot colliding with his big, strong hand. By then my feet were dry and dusty and red, but he hadn't fared much better.

"Haha! You can see my foot on your hand!" I don't think I knew the word imprint quite yet.

"Ahhhh," he must've said in feigned pain, "You got me really good, Lace! Nice job! Auuugh!"

Per usual I would attack him with hugs and emphatically smatter his wide-spread hands with high-fives, in the way that little kids tend to do when they're excited. And he would stumble and fall over whenever I hug-tackled him, likely on purpose because I was so small. I doubt that anyone could have truly knocked him off his feet at that time.

Not me. Not my older sister. Not any of the large dogs in the neighborhood. The only thing he would ever noticeably fear were the gunshots that we always heard outside, and even then, sometimes, he would be stock still and just wait for the noises out the window to dial down.

Besides martial arts (I don't even know what kind it was, only that that was what my dad used to call it), I would do the normal Asian things like learning the piano (only I would do it because it was fun and not because my mom made me). When I was younger, I had fun, and I didn't always intend on going to college when I grew up. I was content with staying home and taking care of my parents and hanging around the community like everyone else. Nothing in Pennyworth is perfect--the cops are racist and the infrastructure's gone to shit and the only bar in town is super run down--but this is home. I like it here, most of the time. My best friend, Blue, lives here. And my sister, Jen, used to spend loads of time with me. And this place was the only place I knew, and my mom and I are okay, and my dad and I were on really good terms before he died, and I had some friendly acquaintances at school.

The reason I lost so many of those things was out of my control. And the town's leadership was to blame for everything that's gone from here now.

I was eight years old when my dad died. He went out in the middle of the night when the police were bothering the gay couple that lives across the street from us. Weedo and

Marshal weren't even bothering the police on purpose, the police just know about them being gay and pick on them for no goddamn reason. When my dad was sneaking out of the house to see his girlfriend across town the police shot him. I don't know why he felt the need to sneak out, except to maybe save face around me, maybe to make me think that he and my mom were happier together than they actually were.

I mean, my mom knew about his girlfriend at this point (at least that's what she tells me). She also told me that dad was never really the type to get married, so her intention was to never follow through with that. Marriage has never been terribly common in Pennyworth anyway, but at this point I can't exactly ask him about his reasoning. I think that she was just being the overly kind person that she is and letting him stay. She also said that she really wanted him to be in my life, so she probably also let him stay here because they had me.

A lot of the people in our neighborhood are people of color, making us one of the more popular places for the police to stop by. What exactly happened, I'll never know. It could've been a race crime, it could've just been the policemen thinking they'd just shot at a raccoon, it could've been because they had a bone to pick with my father. Just because he was white and living where he was, that was enough to piss off a lot of the policemen in town.

It wouldn't at all surprise me if I had told myself that they were just "fireworks" outside my window that night.

That's what I'd told myself about gunshots for a couple of years at that point. I don't even know who'd introduced the idea to me the first time. Maybe my dad. Maybe my mom. Maybe Jen told me. Regardless, I was probably too young to remember and just old enough to start to figure out how to cope.

My dad wasn't just any ordinary guy, not in Pennyworth. He was one of those guys who would take a walk around the block and say "howdy" to everyone he ran into, whether he knew them well or not. He was friends with a lot of people that worked for the mayor, Jeffrey Wheaton. He ate lunch, every day, with people that worked with him at the power plant. He had loads of friends and filled the house with interesting people that would make me laugh and would bring home exciting food that my mom would never make, and my dad could never figure out how to order. He was nearly universally loved, and over half the town came to the funeral we held for him. I'd never seen so many people attempt to squeeze into the teeny church in the center of the town's little plaza. So many people dressed up in their very best clothes to say goodbye to someone that meant the world to me, who meant the world to almost the entire town. There just weren't enough of those poor, broken, wooden pews for everyone. Some people tried to sit on the old gray carpeting, but that ran out of space too.

What's it like to be so missed? Is it foolish to miss someone you can't bring back? Maybe so.

Whenever I started to cry during and after the service, people told me to put my chin up and puff my chest out. Those friends that dad would bring to the house told me to be a tough girl, and that I would never get anywhere if I kept looking back and didn't act strong. I think that by then my sister must've already heard all of the lessons around town for that, that Jen already knew not to cry or to freak out in public anymore. I was only eight, but she was sixteen when the funeral rolled around, and I didn't see a single tear fall. Even if it was my dad that died and not hers, he still loved her like she was his flesh and blood. He still played with her and brought her gifts and took her on adventures. She still missed him a lot, and I heard my sister trying to cry quietly across the room that we shared that night.

Quiet your emotions. Don't tell anyone you're in pain. No one will respect you if they see you cry.

Those were lessons that no one explicitly taught, but everyone still learned to hold onto them for dear life, and to hold on *fast*.

As much as the mayor would like to believe that stifling the appearance of emotional distress of Pennyworth's citizens is doing something to reduce the amount of actual sadness, I know that he can't possibly be right. There's just kind of this encouragement of the mentality that *"everyone is fine except for me, so I'd better blend in."* And now I know that that isn't true, cuz I've heard my mom cry and Jen cry and Blue cry, too. The emotions are still here. But it seems like a lot of people don't know that. And it seems like Mayor Wheaton likes it that way.

When I turned eleven Jen went to college and the house got even quieter than it did before. It wouldn't surprise me if she didn't really want to come back. By this time, my obsession with doing well in school was in full swing. No more piano. I didn't see my sister anymore, just because she doesn't visit home very often. I think she prefers school and life outside of here. Suddenly my mom had more work to do than ever before. Being a schoolteacher has to be really difficult, especially with the underfunding and the overflowing numbers of students.

And the only person I had left was Blue.

Blue's real name is Brigham, and we met when we were in elementary school together. He's really tall now, but when I met him for the first time, he was only slightly taller than I was. He's always been kinda lanky but built? He's black, but he was never told what ethnicity he was. He keeps his hair cropped short and he has a really sharp jaw. Quiet.

He and I were kinda quiet to begin with, but I got even quieter after my dad died. Not a lot of people cared enough to notice, or they were just too smart to get involved with me. If they treated me like something changed, everyone at that school who'd lost a parent to death or (less often) divorce would be treated differently. I wasn't any different. Everyone was taught not to care so I wasn't really hurt by it. Nonetheless, clearly Blue managed to care against the norm.

I couldn't tell if he was really empathetic or if he was truly as sad as I was with my dad's freshly covered grave.

I call him Blue because the first time he talked to me after my dad had died, he came up to me to cheer me up. He challenged me to arm wrestling, and I guess I squeezed his hand so hard for so long that it started to turn blue. He also strained so hard that he kinda started to turn blue in the face. I didn't even win, mostly because I was laughing at the fact that his skin was changing color, but we became friends after that. He had another last name, but I called him Blue so often that people just assumed that I was calling him by his last name, and Brigham Blue he became.

Non-coincidentally, that was the same day that I got into my very first fight. A girl came up to me and told me that it was her father that had killed my dad. It would've been different had she come up to me to apologize, but she had such a smug look on her face, and I could tell she was somehow proud of her father for killing Pennyworth's most favored citizen. I got so mad and was so hyped up by adrenaline that I knocked her over and punched her 'umpteen' times. I know that I got her at least once in the jaw and at least twice in the stomach, and there's no way I got away without a few scratches, but she got the worst of the damage. Because I was so young and because the school was aware of the circumstances, I was only given a week suspension and told to take up something for anger management. Because of that, I returned to martial arts until I started high school. It was nice because it reminded me of my dad, but it'd be a lie if I said I didn't have to fight back tears every once in a while, out of the simultaneous familiarity and change.

Blue was super nice and told me that he would learn martial arts with me if it made me feel better, and so we both learned together how to beat up dummies with our bare and dirty feet, with our little kid-sized hands, in our small and sweaty bodies. Sometimes Jen even joined us when she was free, but I don't think she enjoyed it quite as much as Blue and I did. I don't know what level we were at when we stopped, but we were better than most people we knew. But it's not like there were many outside of the teeny children's class that met once a week in the middle of the hardly used park.

CHAPTER 1

JUMP

——

But now, I'm a senior in high school, and it's the middle of April. Today's the day Brigham brings me to the tallest building. The building is twelve stories high. There are some six- and seven-story buildings across town, but this building is the only one larger than those, and it's the only one that no one can get into, let alone the idea of getting to the top. It's unattainable. It's been abandoned and we haven't had any reason for construction here for over a decade–there's no way we're getting any soon. I think the mayor's too proud to hire professionals except for someone who'll do minor repairs.

The twelve-story used to be a hotel that was supposedly "so fancy it's Heaven!" a few decades ago, before the town got run down. The police boarded it up once the profit started to go down into the negatives and it stopped serving the town any purpose. There are signs up everywhere with things like

"Warning: No Entry" and "No Trespassing". Most people are sure it's all just a hoax and that the police don't give a shit about what happens there, but there's enough superstition that's gone around about barbed wire and traps. Oh well, they might as well pretend that they care about making people aware of potentially crumbling infrastructure, not that they'd do anything if anyone went inside.

Once my mom told me about the hotel, actually. Apparently, after a few dates, she and my dad went to the bar and he got super drunk in front of her. He didn't have a lot of coordination, and he also accidentally told her that he loved her that night. She would always chuckle under her breath and then sigh when she said that bit, the bit about his loving her, but then she would be quiet. She wasn't quite sad, mostly just solemn.

I'm sitting outside my rickety house when Brigham walks his bike up to the tiny porch. He offers his handlebars for me to sit on and kisses my forehead to say hello, and we set off quickly toward the center of town so we'll make it back before my mom comes home from work. Whenever we find a dip Brigham picks up speed and I brace myself, and we jump what feels like three feet into the air. He laughs a lot at it, and I laugh with nerves and relief right along with him. In description it can't be that funny, but in real life it is.

He makes my stomach flutter and hands sting on the way down once we hit the pavement, and on the way down we like to reference *The Dead Poets Society* and release our mighty YAAAAAWWWWWWPS and our own childish guffaws.

"You're an idiot." I don't see his face, but I feel his eyes widen and his lips crack when he smiles at me.

"I know I am, and you love me for it," I say to retort.

"I don't have to, y'know. I could leave you right here and you'd have to walk back without seeing the rooftop at all. I won't even let you follow me to the building; you won't see the way up."

"I can run just as fast as you can ride this bike, you dumbass."

"I never said you couldn't, but who says I'd go without you? Wouldn't be worth the risk with you following me. Maybe now you don't deserve to know what's up there."

I laugh at his mock seriousness and he pedals harder. He has no real reasons to keep secrets from me, right?

"This'll be nice though, won't it?" I ask him. "Before I head to college we'll have a place to hang out whenever I visit."

He kinda just keeps pedaling. We pass the main square with the diner and the church and all the main stores before he starts to talk again. It's not until he clears his throat can I tell that he wants to say something and doesn't really know how. But by then we've completely left any of the main areas of town. We've come close to lots of abandoned buildings and streets. Maybe only a handful of people live in this area. What are we doing here? No one ever comes here just because it isn't practical to invest here, and I didn't know that Blue had this kind of time for exploring. "Y'know you shouldn't visit too often. I don't wanna distract you from school. You shouldn't worry too much about me."

"But I'm always going to worry about you. I love you, and you're my best friend. How could I not? You'd never get in the way of school, Blue. I'm going to visit."

"I don't think you should since I'd get in the way. If you don't visit, I'd get it. I'd still love you."

Time passes uncomfortably for a little after that. There's a sharp pain in my chest and a sting in my eyes. I tell myself it's just the wind making my tears come, and the sharp pain in my chest is just the wind jogging my little boobs up and down. That's all. That is all.

For whatever reason, I catch a picture in my head of Brigham at the top of a roof, on the lip of a raised wall. It's just a memory, the top of some other hotel and him looking back at me like he's excited, just some vacation we went on when we were kids, my mom calling down and telling him not to jump into the pool or he'll break his neck. He's laughing so hard, laughing at the dare I've put him up to and the little scare we're putting on my mom. What a parent, we think, what does she know? It's perfectly safe. And it was.

"Lace." We've made it to the building. I must've blanked out for a moment.

"Blue, I have a bad feeling."

"You didn't answer my question."

"What, what is it?"

"Um, nothing, it doesn't matter."

My throat catches on itself and the bad feeling spreads to my stomach and, oddly enough, to my big toes. But I keep quiet. Brigham wants me quiet. It's fine. It's fine. There's a voice in my head telling me it's wrong, everything is wrong, the next few minutes are crucial, wrong, wrong, wrong... I look up at Brigham and he's shaking. Out of nowhere, he seems a little unsteady.

Eventually, we get to a really tall building. I can tell that it used to be painted a deep green, but the paint is so peeled off that it's mostly just exposed brick work. And there are so many windows that, even though some of them are left open and some of them are just plain broken panes of glass, I start to think about what the different views look like from all of the different heights. Can you see over the wall that surrounds the city from here? What's it like?

"Come on," he says, "We're going up." Instead of walking toward the front of the building, he walks away from me and toward the side of the building to the left of the entrance. When I ask why, he says that the doors on the first level are all too stuck and swelled shut: the paint has stuck to all of the frames. He couldn't pick them open if he tried (which he claimed to have done).

He opens a crate lying on top of a platform two or three feet tall, the crate itself much smaller than the platform. He pulls out a strong, hemp rope and walks closer to the building. I see a window several feet above my head and protruding from it is a metal sort of loop about a foot wide. It must've been used to hang a plant or to connect a clothing line to another building across the street.

Brigham takes aim at the loop with the rope and misses once by what couldn't have been more than an inch. He aims again, a little higher this time, and the rope goes through. I notice for the first time that there is a small something weighing the end of the rope he threw up: smart of Brigham. "I know it's only up to the second story, but down the hall from that room is a stairwell that heads up pretty close to the roof. I'll show you how to get up from there."

He knows I know how to climb a rope, and as he ties the ends at the bottom to two separate hefty crates to keep the rope stable, I think back on the conversation we've been having. Normally when we talk, he sounds comfortable and happy, but since we've stopped at the hotel his voice has gotten solemn. The last time I remember his voice being like this was when his older brother died from a drive-by shooting six months ago. Few people own cars in this town. Mostly just the police. Fuck the police. They're fucking up this town.

I open my mouth to speak and he hushes me. Instead, he starts to hoist himself up toward the window, keeping both hands on the rope to keep his precarious balance. "We'll talk when we get to the roof, alright, Lacey? Make sure you pull the rope up with you before you climb all the way in. There's a trash chute to the right of this window. Drop it down that and it'll drop down into a crate we can access from outside."

"Fine, Blue. Hurry your damn ass up."

He reaches the top quickly and I grapple with the rope for a long moment before putting my weight on the rope completely. As soon as I leap across the windowsill he turns his back on me and tells me to follow him through gritted teeth. I think I hear his voice crack on my name. I hear a quiet sniff coming from his direction. By the time I register how disheveled his demeanor has become and remember I need to move, he's already up half a flight of stairs.

I'd made a mistake believing this would be fun-- he doesn't really wanna talk. Everything feels forced with him, and it feels like I've made him really pissed by asking him about what was wrong and even agreeing to his invitation. I rack my brain as I run up the stairs, two at a time, on my toes, half trying to catch up with him and half trying to stay warm in the cool air.

In the middle of April, it rains a lot. It might be raining now. It is raining now- I hear the thudding following me up the stairs and hitting the brickwork outside. We made it inside just quickly enough to miss the rain and to avoid being pelted by the fat drops.

Why is Brigham angry? What did I do? Was it really just agreeing to come? Did something happen in between the invitation and now? Nothing actually significant comes to mind, nothing I could've done. Nothing but his brother dying on Halloween night, and me ignoring one of his calls last week when he found his brother's old journal and needed to cry. But I didn't really ignore it. Not on purpose. It was just a call I'd missed. Well, not JUST a call, it was THE call for him. All that had happened was there was a field trip I'd forgotten to tell Brigham about. I don't have a cell phone, so he's always called on my home phone. Mama was at work, Jen was at college, and the museum I was at was two towns away.

I didn't forget him. I couldn't ever forget Brigham. I felt guilty on that trip, and I worried about him every moment that I could. He'd rarely given me a reason to be so concerned, but my mind has always jumped to worst case scenarios. I was afraid he wanted someone to stop him from going out to shoot someone or from committing suicide or that he was about to get shot. But those are always my first worries about people when I'm not around. Has Blue ever talked to me about death before? Maybe more than most people I know. Maybe it's because I'm a girl, maybe it's because my dad's already dead, but my mind always leaps to death first.

Leap.

That old memory of Brigham about to jump comes back. I manage a little smile, and I run a little faster in an attempt to feel like it's old times, like everything's fine. I suddenly have to catch up to him. Joy. Happy. Remember. I want to shout and get him to remember too. What's bubbling in my chest?

"Blue! Blue!" I'm not angry anymore. I'm actually kinda scared? Why bring me here and now unless something is about to change? What's going to change? I'm not angry. This is fear.

Below my feet are boards of rickety wood, only slightly different from that of the laminate in my living room and bedroom. For a second I pretend I am at home, that I am not uncertain, that Brigham is only visiting me and we're not on a mad adventure. We've just exited an open window on the twelfth floor, using a fire escape ladder visible on one of the balconies, the walls overgrown with ivy and cobwebs. There's a lipped-up wall a couple feet higher than the rest of the rooftop. Up here it's cold and still raining, large PLOPS hitting my head kind of violently unless I stand under a shallow awning. There's a single table, a patio umbrella that's deteriorating, teetering with the rain, and a few broken foldable chairs. Pulled up to the table are two small, sturdy crates sitting on top of the concrete.

"Blue?" He's been staring at me since I've made it up from the twelfth story balcony. If it's possible, he's made it through the window and onto the roof faster than he made it onto the second story. The rain slows me down and makes the rusting ladder slippery, but he didn't seem to care at all, like it was nothing to him. I took my time on the way up, remembering to take comfort in a few things: Brigham wants me here, there's a mattress on this balcony (however old) that looks like it'll catch our fall, I haven't had nearly enough time with my best friend in a long time. "Blue?" I ask again. He hasn't said a word.

It feels like I'm crying, but I'm unsure because the rain is falling on me so thickly. I know that my short sleeves and jean shorts are not enough for this weather. The water on my face is hot, but my arms and my legs are freezing; I am crying. And as I cry, I shiver like a dog. Brigham quickly walks over to me, but how he travels so many yards away from the ladder we entered from I don't know. He's swift and just as swiftly takes off his letterman jacket, the one his brother used to let him borrow. He slips it over my shoulders and kisses my forehead again. I know that he's cold because now his arms are bare, and all he's wearing now are jeans and a grey muscle shirt. I say his name again, this time steadily "Blue."

"Hey, Lace." He finally answers. "Lace, I'm sorry. I'm sorry that I brought you here and that it's raining and it's freezing." He's crying and laughing at the same time as he talks. "I'm sorry that I'm not better for you and that you couldn't be friends with someone better— smarter or tougher or whatever." He grabs at his hair with his hand and it looks a mess when he pulls it away.

"Blue, you don't need to be sorry for this shit, okay? You don't have to be sorry for anything." And now I'm laughing and crying too. "You're great, okay? I love you and you're amazing."

"Lacey, I'm not amazing." He scoops me into a hug, my head fitting comfortably under his chin. I can feel the stubble on his chin scratching against my scalp. "I haven't been honest about anything. I haven't even been honest with myself." He shuffles through the contents of his jacket pockets, the one he's just put over me. He pulls out a single piece of notebook paper that's obviously been folded and refolded umpteen times, and he hands it over to me. "Take this, turn your back to me, and read it."

At that point he stood there behind me, but as my back turned around, I heard him walk and take slow steps away from me toward the lip of the wall, away from the corner with the ladder and the balcony and the mattress. He doesn't wanna leave yet, maybe he wants to talk. I open the note and read with my heart pumping fast and hard.

Dear Lacey,
I wanna die...

There's a lot more he's written, but I drop it onto the wood beneath my feet before I even get the chance to think about what's coming next. I have to turn around, I have to ask him why he feels this way, I can't believe he's confiding in me with this stuff because he's rarely been so vulnerable before. When I turn around, I see him standing up on the wall with his back to me, and he's shaking. And the next few seconds feel like they take forever, like I'm not going to make it over to him in time. And I run to him. And I yell that he can't. And I can only barely hear myself yell because I can only hear my heart and how loudly the rain is yelling in my ears. By the time I make it to the wall he braces himself likes he's about to jump. But he stops and starts to turn himself around. For a split second, I think he's going to come down and he's rethinking it all, but he's still bracing himself.

I don't know if he was just going to fall back because he couldn't bear to watch the ground hurdle toward him, or if he's actually going to come back onto the roof and break down and cry in front of me. I don't know at all, because all I do is grab him by both legs and pull down toward me. Hard.

I feel his body raise for a moment before it pulls back and falls on top of me. In midair, as I pull, his body turns 180 degrees and I hear a loud thud and what I hope isn't a crack as he hits the back of his head against the lip of the wall he was standing on two seconds before. He did jump. He'd just started to, but I got him. He's not gone.

I don't know how hard his head has hit against the concrete. The thud was hard.

For a moment all I focus on is how the brickwork on the wall's lip was once painted green but has now started peeling. The brick is mostly exposed, and it's much prettier than the green that's left, especially in the rain. Why has brickwork never looked this nice before? Why can't I pull my focus onto anything else for a moment and a half?

Luckily his legs hit the ground first, and most of his body lands on top of my body. When I scramble out from under him I look at his head, which has started bleeding from the impact. I take off the jacket and ignore the cold- I've stopped feeling it- and use it to prop up his head. I grab the bottom of my top and rip hard, breaking off a couple of strips to use to staunch the bleeding. I watch the yellow change to orange. From the front pocket of his jeans I grab his cell phone and hit to the emergency button. I watch his face start to pale a little and try to look away from the orange changing to a deep red.

They answer almost instantly, within a half ring I hear "Hello, what's your emergency?"

"I need help. I'm at the top of the abandoned hotel in Pennyworth, my best friend just tried to jump off... No, he's still with me... Yes, I stopped him... He hit his head when I pulled him down onto the roof... How quickly can you get here?"

CHAPTER 2

OUTSIDE

—

Blue works at a run-down diner in the little plaza at the center of town, a couple of doors down from the church where my dad had his funeral. The truck stop kind of place that you'll see in a lot of movies is exactly like this place, only the chairs are a little more ripped than usual and the jukebox only works if you hit it a couple of times. Also, the jukebox isn't for aesthetics as much as it's the only thing the owner could get his hands on.

There's semi-cracked black and white tiling on the floors. The walls are a dingy, used-to-be-white yellow, and on those there are some pretty racy pictures of women on what looks like blown up magazine covers, but I don't recognize who most of them really are. I see the names and get lost. They look pretty, though. Sometimes it makes me feel funny, not being straight like everyone around me. But they're pretty.

It's not very often that we get the opportunity to get things from out of town, and just a singular computer in the library has access to the internet. Not that that's much of an issue for us, most of the people in Pennyworth like the small-town vibes and that's why they live here. It's not even too far out from slightly larger towns that have substantial hospitals and grocery stores and Starbucks® with free Wi-Fi.

The diner where Blue works used to be a popular stop for truckers, but the roads have been updated to run farther away from town. Now it's mostly a place for kids from the high school to hang out after school hours, to buy burgers and fries and milkshakes. On occasion, we'll get someone out of town visiting because of the functional rest-stop-ishness of the place, but we don't see unfamiliar faces very often.

The library, the church and the diner are all in this main hub of the town. This is where most people work at their day jobs unless they either have permits for working outside of the city or they work at one of the schools on various edges of town. My mom has to drive all the way across town from where we live every morning to get to her teaching job. I think that's just because we would have an impossible time trying to live anywhere near the white neighborhoods, but she seems fine with it. It's not like Pennyworth is even that big, so the drive isn't bad.

The buildings in the main hub are all kinda run down, except for some of the more expensive ones that can afford the upkeep on their infrastructure. That kind of upkeep certainly isn't the norm, though. The streets could be more cracked. The paint could be fresher, but it's certainly nicer than my neighborhood.

Sometimes when we spend time at the diner, like when I'm waiting for Blue to get off work, I just people watch and see who comes in. I like to hope for people who don't come in often so I can imagine their lives, and even with the people I don't know very well I wonder what they do. How different can they be from me? Most of them aren't chinks and a lot of them don't plan on going to college, yet they still stay in school. What's it like at home? Have they gone on more vacations than I have? How difficult is that to do with border patrol? Are they going to be part of the police force in Pennyworth when we're all grown up?

And, with the people coming from out of town or for those who aren't around very often, I always hope that there's a woman in the vicinity. Maybe in her forties or early fifties, maybe with kids, maybe married, but not any of those things definitively. But the only reason I hope for that is because I'm always hoping that I'll make eye contact with the woman my dad was dating. But he told me so little about her. What color is her hair? In the last nine, almost ten, years has she moved out of town? How confidently does she stand? Any woman who could've drawn my father's eye after my mom must've been confident. Either that or she was really special in some other capacity. Could she sing? Does she have a dancer's body? Is she an artist? A teacher? Or maybe she doesn't work. Did she and my dad have kids together? I'm sure I wasn't his first kid. Why would I be his last?

But that's my worrying about someone's life that ended almost a decade ago. My dad isn't around, and this woman had no connection to me when he was alive. Maybe he liked to keep it that way, separate every woman he'd ever loved, if he even loved them, all of the children he'd ever had, from the new life he was making for himself in slightly new places around the state. Even if he didn't love my mom, he had to have loved me at least a little bit, or why else would he stick around for eight years plus a pregnancy?

Maybe it ceased to matter at all as soon as he died. As far as I know, nothing of his love life was ever illegal and none of it should scare me. He was around me for as long as he could've been, right up until he died. It doesn't matter. Or maybe it does, but I feel like it shouldn't. I don't want it to. All that I want to matter is that Brigham is alive and that he still matters. As long as you don't die you don't cease to matter. The past doesn't matter. All that matters is now.

But how can I say that? If it weren't for the past, Blue wouldn't be in the hospital. That's how we got here. That's part of why he wanted to die, part of how we became friends. Would Brigham and I even be friends if my dad were alive? I'd like to hope so, since we were both so quiet and were near each other so often in elementary school. But maybe that would've sealed it, too. We were both too quiet to speak to each other much until my dad did die. I'm not glad that my dad died, but I am glad that Brigham is around and still alive in front of me. Does one outweigh the other? I don't think they could. If Brigham died would there be someone else who became close friends with me as a result of it? There's no way of knowing, and I'd rather not know.

I guess we haven't experienced a lot of things out of Pennyworth because of the big wall that surrounds it. I think a lot of people might've thought a lot about trying to get outside of the walls at the city limits, but it was never a big goal of mine. Pennyworth was the only place I'd ever been to, and I guess I didn't think that anything would ever be any different outside of there, and all of the people that I actually cared about were already on the inside of the border wall.

The wall itself is mostly concrete, and it's several feet tall. When you approach it, you can see that it used to be painted with a thick coat of bright white paint, but now it's also really chipped and dirty and faded all over.

At the points where the wall breaks there are big fences and gates patrolled by some of the policemen. They're mostly idle because not a lot of people hang out by the border. There just isn't enough to do over there and everyone is pretty pre-occupied with work and school.

I think that there are only a few of these points where people can come in and out. They're maybe four or five of them tops, and one of those opens so that people have access to the beach, even though it's rarely used. Well, it mostly has the illusion of being open. A lot of the beach is still encapsulated by wall that wraps around it. Even if you wanted to escape from the beach gate, you'd have to go out to sea pretty far so that the patrol police don't see you. Luckily, the wall does very little to disturb the view out there. The wall is set so far back that there's a good several miles of beach where you still can't see the wall. There's an illusion that there isn't a wall to even keep you in.

We went through another one of the exits, facing the opposite direction from the opening that leads to the beach, leading to a town that I don't know the name of. The town that holds the aforementioned hospitals and coffeeshops and grocery stores and free wi-fi. The process for getting in and out doesn't seem complicated from here. We need to go out of town to the hospital and we have police escorts, so they let us through without questioning us too much. I guess you have to have a job outside the city limits or some other legitimate reasons to get outside. I don't know all of the complicated inner workings of it, but I know we make it outside.

The first thing I did when Brigham and I made it to the hospital was sit in the waiting room. Everything was oddly inviting. The waiting room had cushy sofas and chairs, an area with those doctor's office children's toys, and a little table with a vase of white roses was in the corner. It still smelled like a normal hospital. It smelled a little like bleach and— y'know how cold kinda has a smell?— it smelled like cold. There were sounds of pleasant conversation coming from the reception desk, even when we had to rush Blue in through the doors— how oddly calming.

When the nurse finally came out to speak with me, I braced myself for the worst. When she told me that he was still alive, I cried of relief. If there were a hospital in Pennyworth, would the nurse have told me to stop crying because I looked foolish? She didn't do it here though. Is this normal? I know that Mayor Wheaton would've tried to make a change with it as soon as possible had he known about this. Are there even any slogans about positivity associated with this town?

The next thing I did was ask if I could see him. She told me that his condition still had to stabilize. There were nominal scrapes all over his back and across the backs of his legs, but worse than that was the blow to the head that he suffered. There was no way to know that he'd hit his head as hard as he did when I pulled him down from the lip at the top of the roof, and I couldn't have thought about how much it actually hurt him in the midst of pulling him. He landed basically on top of me. I thought he'd be safer. Maybe the shock was still too much on his head. Maybe his head made contact with the concrete harder than I had initially heard. I saw the blood though. I should've been aware already. I should've known how badly I'd fucked up. I fucked up. My mind is going dark places as she fills me in, tells me that he'll be all right to be discharged tomorrow in the afternoon, they just want to run some tests to see if he should be referred to a therapist or put on depression meds or go into a mental hospital.

But that's not the point I think to myself, *he's alive because of what I did.* That's what matters right now. *She said he'll be okay tomorrow everything will be back to normal.*

They won't let me in to see him for another hour, but it's getting later and later, almost eight o'clock and I haven't eaten anything in hours.

"Is there any way that I can have something to eat, then? I won't be able to go back to Pennyworth without Brigham."

"I suppose that'll be alright, but I suppose you'll also need a place to stay. If need be you can stay in the room with Mr. Mathis overnight."

Mr. Mathis? Oh. I always forget that Mathis is Brigham's last name. Everyone I know has always called him Brigham or Blue or Brigham Blue. No one's used his real last name in years. Not in school, not around town, only on official forms of identification are there traces of his last name. The nurse looks confused when I'm surprised at Brigham's last name, but I don't think she realizes it's the last name that confuses me.

"Oh don't be concerned about staying in there with him. We have guest beds we can pull in for you, some pillows and blankets. I know it's a little sparse, but you'll be plenty comfortable in there. He's been transferred from the ER to the psychological facility. Lights are out at 10:30 for patients."

"Oh, yes, thank you. That'd be great. Can you show me where to go?"

"I'll have an intern take you to Patient Family Dining. Mr. Mathis is in room..." she takes a moment to look at the paperwork in her hands, "room 407, right down the hall a little ways from the dining hall."

I give her a nod of thanks at the hospitality, and it's only then that I realize how expensive the stay in this hospital is going to be. I'm going to be staying in his room with him, borrowing supplies that have to be washed, on top of the care that needs to be paid off in the ER.

I'll take up an extra job or something by the beginning of summer, I think to myself, *and maybe I'll ask my mom for help to help pay it off.*

"Actually," I say, "just the meal and a blanket will be fine. I don't need much other than that. I'll check up on Brigham around 9 o'clock, if that's all right."

She takes some notes down on her clipboard about what I've said and then nods me off to a cute, little blonde girl with springy hair that bounces when she walks. The intern has her hair tied up in a high ponytail and has slightly overdone her makeup, but overall, she's very pretty and cordial enough. She seems oddly happy here, about my age. I've never seen her before, but I get the odd feeling that she's popular wherever she goes to school. I especially get the feeling that we'd be friends if I knew her, but that I'd secretly jealous of her blonde hair and the spring in her step. I would've tried to talk to her, but she drops me off at the dining hall very promptly, and with a "have a good night now" she scurries off for her next task.

Despite the bougie-ness of the hospital, the hospital food is pretty bland and dry. No one else in the dining hall seems to mind this, though, and I don't quite mind either. All I can think about is the fact that *Blue is alive. Blue is alive. Blueisalive. Blueisalive. BlueisaliveisaliveisaliveBlueisalive.*

And it seems so extra to think like that, to only think about how excited I am for my best friend to be alive and that I get to keep him. All of the other people in this room may not have that luxury. They all seem kind of solemn and serious, they all seem worried like they don't know what's going to be happening to the people they really care about. In the midst of all this not knowing, I feel like the only one that knows enough to sustain myself.

When nine o'clock finally rolls around, I stand up and head to room 407. I know that the nurse says that the room is meant to be close to the dining hall, but the trip there feels like a journey. It's one of those long treks that you'd take to get through the Himalayan Mountains, or through the desert of Death Valley, or something else equally as long and terrifying as those two.

It feels like a walk of dread, but it shouldn't be. Blue is alive, and I don't have to worry about it. I might be able to talk to him, whether he could talk to me or not. Right now, the biggest question in my mind is my wondering about whether he'll be conscious or not when I get there. I need to talk to him about what happened this afternoon, but that conversation will be terrifying. Will it be worse if he's awake or asleep? If he stays asleep then no one gets hurt anymore, for the time being. No one opens up the chasm of feelings that comes out of an afternoon like this. If he stays asleep maybe he'll remember it all as a dream. If he stays asleep and I fall asleep fast, maybe I'll wake up and find out that none of today really happened. That's not how you reach the roof of the tallest building in town. That's not the color a yellow t-shirt turns when you use it to staunch blood flow. That's not how hospital food tastes.

But if he's awake, I find out a little bit faster what's been going on through his mind. I get to read the suicide note in front of him, the way that he wanted me to do. I'll get to see how not dead he really is, with his eyes open and his mouth moving and his voice making guttural laughing sounds into the cold air of the hospital. Maybe the realness of it all won't matter, because I'll know how to fix it. I'll know how to keep it all from happening again, and how to make him happy, and how to keep him around for as long as I can, and what went wrong and how it went wrong and…

Room 407 is small but somehow cozy. There's a small armchair and an end table with a package of baby wipes and a lamp that emits a warm light. There's a plastic plant in the corner and a small window above his bed. He looks comfortable enough, and there's a warmness in the air that fights the usual coldness of hospitals. The nurse that spoke to me earlier is there to greet me, and she does so cheerily. I watch her carefully using a baby wipe to wipe off some dry blood from the back of his head.

She points to a couple of blankets on the armchair and a blow-up mattress that's in the corner, and as she does this, she walks toward me and whispers, "don't worry about the extra charge on the bedding, okay? I've got it covered."

I try to stop her and tell her not to do that, but she scurries out before I can say anything. And Brigham is in the room and I have to look at him. It's been hours since I have, and the last time that I saw him was when the EMT loaded us both into the back of the ambulance and booked it here. He looked less than wonderful then, blood everywhere and all scraped up and not able to open his eyes. When I walked in at first, he was asleep, but he'd begun to wake up as the nurse spoke to me and told me not to worry about the extra charge.

When she leaves, Blue tells me, "Her name is Gracie, I think. She's been taking really good care of me." He even manages a smile when he says that he feels cared for, but only briefly before his face goes melancholy.

I try and smile back, "That's good." I can tell that they've changed his bandages, and it looks like he's taken a bath. His hair is wet from being washed and he's wearing a hospital gown instead of his street clothes, but little else has changed since I've pulled him down.

I see his Letterman jacket hanging off his headboard. "Did they wash your Letterman already?"

"Yeah, Gracie even offered to try and get it ironed, but I told her not to worry about it."

My yellow shirt is a crop top now, and I'm still in my short jean shorts.

When I mention it, he guesses that I'm cold, and he reaches for the letterman to hand it to me. "Are you cold, Lace? Here, you can wear it."

"No, it's okay," I try to stop him, but he hands it to me with nominal effort. It's clear that he's sore and tired, but he's just as stubborn as he's always been. When I take it and put it on, I watch his eyes start to fill up with remembrance for his brother and the day's events, both.

"My brother is already dead," he seemed to realize momentarily, "and I would be too."

I don't think Blue would never admit it, but I think he feels like his brother has betrayed him for dying. Has he made the connection yet? I'd have lost him and maybe I would've felt betrayed at the loss of my best friend. He motions me closer to the side of the bed so I can be closer to his face.

"Blue, I'm so glad you're alive. I don't know what I would've done if I lost you, you asshole." I give him a light slap on his exposed bicep, and then I feel my own eyes fill up with tears and glaze over.

He opens his arms wide and envelops me in a mix of soap scented flesh and hospital gown paper and wet eyes.

"I, uh, I haven't re--" my voice catches on my throat before it can make its way out completely. I don't know how to say I haven't read the letter yet without saying it outright, and it's a couple of breaths before I can speak at all.

I cough a couple of times before I manage to say, "I haven't read the letter yet, I don't have to if you don't want me to."

"Can you please read it, for me?" he urges me to read it in front of him, out loud if it makes it easier for me. And so I start. He says the words along with me, like he'd memorized it and read it over and over again before he decided what he was doing was final. For a split second, I wonder what made him decide he wanted to die in front of me instead of alone, but I tell myself it doesn't matter and just start to read.

Dear Lacey,

I wanna die. I'm killing myself. I know that it's a shock, but I'm terrified, and I know you must be terrified too. But I don't think I can go to college; my life just feels like it isn't made for that. I'm made to be a fuck up, and I know I'm just destined for a dead end like everyone else we know. That is, everyone but you. You're insanely smart and talented, Lace, and I don't want you to waste it by living under me as someone to look up to.

I know that I'm like a brother to you, especially since your sister hasn't been around for a while and your dad's been "away" and your mom's always at work. And I love you madly because you're the best little sister I've ever had. I know you're the only sibling I've had since I've lost my brother, but I don't think you could've been better.

You're growing up, and I just don't want to turn you into a failure by being a failure myself. I'd be a poor example, and I don't care about anyone else, and I know no one else really cares about me. I think it'd be best to get rid of me, to get out of your life and to get out of my own before I can screw it up anymore.

For the past few months, I've felt like a failure. I haven't been good enough to stick it out to go to college, and I dropped out of high school. I've been planning this jump for a couple of weeks. I know that I'm stupid for never bringing it up to you, but you always seem happy. It was never the right time to break your happiness, even though I know your whole life you've been forced to be stronger than that.

I guess as I take the plunge, I hope you'll forgive me. I just want a life that's out of your way. I just don't want to be a bother to anyone in Pennyworth anymore. And if I don't find better prospects, I guess I deserve that.

The excuses I gave were pretty lame, I know, but most of the sadness has been inexplicable aside from feeling like I've been restricting you to this place. On top of that, I know no one would miss me beside you. I guess I'm still secretly wishing that you'll talk me out of this, but I guess since you're reading this I either didn't let you try, or I was just too stubborn to listen to you and believe I should stay. In all likelihood, I probably just didn't let you try.

Bury me quietly outside of town and tell everyone that I skipped town, that I won't be coming back. I promise you I'm giving you this goodbye because I love you, Lacey. I think I also want to die because I don't want to live without you around when you're in college, even though I know you'll be doing incredible things. Believe me, okay? God, I love you.

Love, Brigham

And I look at him, and he looks at me, and we make eye contact. He knew every word before I'd opened the page, and we're both crying again. By now it's almost ten o'clock and I only have half an hour before lights are out. Time would be better spent filling the air mattress and getting ready to sleep somehow, but instead I walk over and kiss him on the forehead. And I tell him over and over again he's not in the way of me while he fights against me. And I tell him that I'd feel as awful as he did when his brother died, and that I'm glad that he's alive, and that he's not allowed to try to die anymore.

Maybe bringing up his brother was a dumb idea, but I would've felt that way. I would've missed him as much as he misses his brother now. Am I making him feel guilty by making him think about the consequences of his trying to kill himself and being successful?

All that I can remember is the first time Blue told me about Donte dying, how it was obviously a drive by shooter based off of the new tire skid marks and the bullet holes in Donte's body, how much he wishes he could've been there to help him. Donte wasn't even asking to die young, and he was stuck there just dying by himself for so long. We still don't know who it was that shot him. We don't know if they were being racist or they mistook him for someone else or if Donte really had someone out for him. We don't know. But so few people have cars besides the police: it's hard not to assume.

"If you're gonna die, you have to let me die first, okay? That way I can't miss you too much" I tell him while I ruffle his thick curls and draw circles on his dark skin with my thumb. By the time 10:30 hits and the lights are off, he never once looks like he believes me.

He looks like he realizes how badly I'd truly be hurt, but he's in disbelief about the idea that his being dead would hurt me as much as I say it would.

Right before lights go out, he starts to speak, "Lacey." I start to walk over to the air mattress in the dark, the one Gracie left for me.

"I need you to know, I never want to hurt you the way Donte hurt me when he died. That sucks, but I didn't really let myself think about that until now."

"I know. And Blue, I need you to know that you've never held me back," I begin to reference his letter, "But I'd rather you hold me back than live without you. I think living without you would hold me back too. You might as well stay here." I'm half crying when I say this, and I take a deep breath and let out a slightly too loud, monosyllabic laugh of relief.

And then he chuckles. And then there's a silence for a little while.

"Hey," he seems to change speed, "Can I tell you something? It's kinda negative, but I feel like I should."

"Sure, Blue, what's up?"

"I wanted to tell you about the first time that I tried to kill myself. I haven't told anyone before because I never felt like I could, and I haven't let myself think about it in a long time, but I feel like I should."

I take a deep breath and sigh before nodding, "Sure, whatever you want. I'm here for you, whatever you wanna talk about."

"It'll be pretty descriptive. I think I've thought about it too much. Eh heh. So uhh," He clears his throat, "I was in my bedroom and I was lying in bed. I could hear my dad outside, and the TV was up really loud, and he was drunk. Because the TV was up so loud, I knew that he wouldn't be able to hear me if I started to struggle, and he was so conked out I knew that he wouldn't come in to check on me even if he could hear.

"I put my face into my pillow and for a little bit I could still breathe. It was rank, like the green pillowcase was brimming with sweat that couldn't be washed out. But, I remember, I'd washed it the day before by hand in the kitchen sink. I really didn't wanna breathe, so I pushed my face down harder so that the pillowcase was pulled taut across my mouth and my nostrils were smashed closed. And I just lay there, and for a couple minutes I couldn't think about anything else. My dad was outside getting drunk and mindlessly watching TV.

That was his way of escaping all of the painful shit that he was dealing with, with not having my mom around and having to provide for me somehow and not really being able to find any work in town or in the surrounding areas. That's why he's drunk all the time. I bet he could've gotten a job had he tried, but I think he was so defeated by everything that was going on that he just didn't. He didn't even try.

"Part of me pushed my face so far down into that pillow because I wanted to die. But the rest of me, which was a lot of me actually, was just kinda hoping that he would notice and care about what was going on. I'd tried to tell him that things were wrong, but I could never tell if he even cared even when he was sober. And when he was drunk—well I've never bothered to tell him much of anything when he was incapacitated like that. What would the point be when he wouldn't be able to do anything or even remember in the morning?

"I remember that I was crying really hard. When I'm at home, even now, I feel really lonely. My dad is still there, sitting on the couch, watching TV or just leaving the TV on if he's fallen asleep, and he's almost always drunk when I'm home. I was tired of feeling so alone, like there was no point in coming home if there was no one to talk to. That's part of why I'm always working at the diner or trying to hang out with you. Because if I go home, I'm alone again."

Before he can keep going, he starts to cry. And I mean a really ugly, full cry. I've never seen him like this before.

I don't think he's ever let himself look like this in front of me before.

"I think the last time I cried this hard," he refers to the present, "was that night. I was crying so hard because I was tired of feeling alone. I was crying so hard because all that I wanted was something to distract myself that wasn't booze because I mean, look at how fucked up my dad is. I was crying so hard because I needed someone to talk to about anything and I couldn't talk to about it with anyone. Every teacher who had ever seen me crying just told me to keep my chin up, everyone that I ran into at the diner, everyone that I ran into anywhere. They all just told me to keep my chin up. And I think that they felt badly about it, but they also didn't want policemen to see anything. They didn't wanna get in trouble. They didn't wanna see me in trouble. If they shamed me out of crying, then no one had to deal with it.

"My face might've gone blue at some point, but I couldn't really know for sure because everything was black with my eyes staring straight into the pillow. Or were my eyes closed? It wouldn't have mattered in any case because there was nothing for me to see. My face looked like it was a different color later on though, when I finally had the chance to look into the mirror. My lights are kinda orange at home, so that could've warped the way I saw things, but I had one of those little stand up mirrors on my desk next to my bed, y'know the one that's dark brown and doesn't really match the light wood on my bed frame? But I think that I looked blue.

"And my dad never walked in. And I don't know why I picked my face up out of the pillow other than I thought that I couldn't do that to you, like Donte had done to my dad and me. And for some reason I knew that something would be worth it at some point. At least I hoped it would be."

It all just tumbles out of him. This is the most my best friend has ever told me about himself, ever. And he just kept going. He almost couldn't stop. He'd been dying to say this for a really long time, dying to say it to anybody.

I stumble out of the air mattress I'm in and grope the air in front of me until I find his hospital bed frame. As I climb up onto the mattress and beside him, I wrap my arms around his body, hoping the pressure doesn't hurt him too much. He does the same.

"Thank you for telling me, Blue. I love you."

"I love you too, Lacey."

I lie there silently for a moment. I'm contemplating what he's just told me, letting it sink in. "Do you think it is worth it?" I finally ask him.

"Not hurting you makes it worth it. Right now feels worth it, y'know?"

I nod into his chest. "Yeah, I think I do know."

We lie there like that for a little while, with both of our arms wrapped around each other. And we're comfortable, really comfortable.

We stay there until he tells me that I should get some sleep, and then I climb back down and land softly on the air mattress.

He sends me a gruff "goodnight" from his side of the room.

And I say, "Goodnight, Blue."

I think he's snoring before he can even hear me.

CHAPTER 3

HOT CHOCOLATE

———

I wake up at roughly two o'clock in the morning, and Blue is snoring really loudly. I try to remember some information from a psychology class I took last year: did snoring mean you actually weren't sleeping very well? I figure it probably doesn't matter that much. After all, this isn't the first time he's has woken me up in the middle of the night with his snoring, and he's been fine for this long. But, from experience, I know I won't be able to fall asleep again now that I've been woken up.

His testing for depression will be starting in the morning, and he won't be discharged until tomorrow afternoon. What if he isn't diagnosed with it even after all of this? Or worse, what if the recommended treatment is more expensive than we can afford? Could we afford pills? Ones that don't make him more likely to kill himself, unlike those warnings on television commercials? Would we be able to afford a therapist that doesn't suck ass? I mean therapy works really well for some people, but the ones in Pennyworth are notorious for having no idea what the fuck they're doing. Would we be able to afford bills that come along with being admitted to a mental hospital? Would he even let me help him pay for things? Certainly, his dad would never help. His dad is hardly ever sober. This is gonna have to be something that goes under the table.

Still stuck in a spiral of questions, I've snuck into the hallway of the hospital and trying to remember my way out. Nurses are walking around, essentially patrolling the rooms to make sure the patients don't get out. A handful of them are halfway running as new patients get admitted, but for the most part it's calm. One makes eye contact with me and I mutter that I'm trying to find the restroom. He points me down the hall that leads to the lobby, and I hurry to make it into the ladies' room before anyone else looks at me strangely. While I'm in the restroom I pull out the note again, read it over a couple of times in the dull light of the bathroom, and ponder its contents.

The page has clearly been folded over and over again, so some of the pen marks have started to display wear. I can't help noticing that the bottom of the page is the residency to a few tear-smeared letters. I don't know if they're my own, from when I read the letter aloud with Brigham, or if Brigham cried over it while he was writing it. It's difficult to imagine that they're his tears, considering his careful handwriting and lack of scratched out words. He wanted his last letter to me to be perfect, he wanted to look as sure of himself as he possibly could in his decision as he presented it to me. He worked hard to keep the shakiness out of his lettering, as the writing seems tighter than the typical writing I see from him. He stifled himself to look this controlled to me.

My eyes well up looking at it all over again. He stifled himself and all of his emotions while he thought that he was stifling me and my ability to go to college (though it'd just be community college, anyway) in the future. It's nice to hear from him that he thinks I'm made for great things, but it's awful to hear that he believes the opposite to be true for himself. He wants to go to school with me, but he doesn't have the money to support himself, and he doesn't think that he's smart enough for it. A long time ago he told me that he doesn't think that he'd be worth a slot at a community college because he'd be taking opportunity away from someone who actually mattered. I wish he'd understand that he does matter.

That's what baffles me. He knows full well that he has the ability to be successful and support himself. He knows that going to college would be a great way to take care of himself. But he still thinks that other people deserve success more than he does. He thinks that a positive change for himself means that someone else, someone who deserves it more, will be stuck with something negative. He thinks that he takes up too much space. He thinks that doesn't deserve positive opportunity. He thinks that mattering to anyone takes up too much time and energy from other people, and that's what breaks my heart.

Part of me wants to go outside and sleep in a somewhere because I won't be able to fall asleep here, but most of me really knows that if I ditch Blue at the hospital he'll be lost and confused as to where I've gone. If I leave him a note, he'll blame himself for my not sleeping well, or he'll wish that I were there waiting for him while he was being tested. Even if the former is somewhat (okay, very) true, the latter severely outweighs the truth of it.

I walk to the front check-in desk in the lobby and I ask the nurse (oddly, the same one from this afternoon) there if I can go outside and take a quick walk, that I'm staying overnight with a patient and I'll be back within the hour. She writes patient and guest information on a notepad and hands it to me. "Show this to me or to Shelley on your way back in, we'll let you back into the room as long as you're back before eight AM this morning." Gracie gives me a weary but happy smile. She loves doing her job here, I can tell, but it's also clear that she doesn't take many breaks.

"I know what it's like in Pennyworth, honey, I've lived there quite a while. Take all the time you need, okay?"

"Thank you so much. I didn't know you lived in Pennyworth too. I'm so thankful for all of the help, even though I know I haven't been the easiest guest to deal with, I'm sure. How long have you lived in Pennyworth?"

"Just over a decade. I came to town because I had a boy-friend that lived there. Of course we're not together anymore, but I like it for the most part. I like how small it feels, how middle-of-nowhere I get to be. The police situation could be a little bit better, but you win some and you lose some, right?"

"Really? That's a long while! I hope to see you around the diner sometime. It'd be nice to treat you to a shake at some point, for everything that you've done to help today."

"I think I've seen you there a couple of times before, actually. Mr. Mathis has taken my order at the register a lot of the time, and sometimes he serves my food to me. I'd really like for us to get together.

"Thank you, Gracie. I'll be back really soon!"

I head outside without knowing where I'm heading. Maybe I'll just take a walk around the block and see what stores and restaurants are around. Maybe instead of going to the diner for lunch tomorrow, we'll go to a place we've never been before and make an adventure out of it. We won't have to go back home right away, and we can forget about how we got here, why we came and what we're doing. Take a baby wipe to it all, like Gracie did with Blue's blood before.

Depression.

Baby wipe.

Dead father.

Baby wipe.

Dead brother.

Baby wipe.

Racist cops.

Baby wipe.

College.

Baby wipe.

All of fucking Pennyworth.

Baby. Fucking. Wipe.

I imagine us eating at a restaurant, one of those ones with pre-packaged soups and bread-bowls and grilled cheeses and artisan potato chips. I imagine us going to a karaoke bar and scream-singing into microphones the kinds of songs that make us laugh. Us getting licenses and getting real cars to drive. Buying an apartment together and watching those tv shows that, for lack of cable, we've never gotten to see. I really just imagine changing everything, watching the two of us getting married and going on double dates and finding jobs we love without having to try so hard.

And then I fade back. Even if that kind of life is a dream for the two of us, we'd never be able to attain it. Not now. Not as high schoolers, not with a background from Pennyworth. Even if we lived in this town, just the next town over, we'd have so much more opportunity. Pennyworth is just that cut off from everything. Not even Gracie was able to get everything that she should've. She has a job, but she hasn't gotten everything she clearly deserves. My mom couldn't get it. I wonder if Jen could get it. Is that why she's in school so many states away? Can you only be so successful in big cities?

I step inside one of those 24-hour coffee shops and eye the thousand item menu for something I'd be able to find at the diner. If I asked for a black coffee would they look at me oddly? With so many exciting drinks would they be surprised? Would it make more sense to get hot chocolate? Or should I try something different? Maybe I'm not ready for that. I walk up to the cash register and a pretty blonde girl smiles at me.

"What can I get started for you?"

"Can I get a hot chocolate?"

"What size?"

"Umm, a medium I guess?" Why does she look like I've said something odd?

She grabs a cup for me and says "Alright, a grande hot chocolate. Will that be all?"

"Oh, uh yeah! Can I use your bathroom?"

"Of course! The number is taped above the code box!"

Her cheeriness feels fake but oddly compelling. And it flusters me a little bit. Maybe it's real and I just can't imagine the saturation of that happiness being that possible. Could that be the case? Or is it actually fake?

I walk into the apparently single-stall restroom and stare at myself in the mirror while I pee. This is how I've been walking around. My hair is frizzy and unbrushed, my shirt and shorts are disheveled, and I can see the entirety of my left shoulder. The barista didn't look at me like I'd said something odd. She looked at me like I looked odd. Maybe she looked concerned? Or disgusted? Or just like she was try-ing not to laugh? I couldn't really tell. She played it off so well.

When I flush, I stand in front of the mirror and try to flatten my hair out and brush out some of the tangles with my fingers. I adjust my shirt to cover up my bra strap and both my shoulders, and I try in vain to pull it down and cover some more of my stomach. When that doesn't work, I pull up my shorts as high as I can without giving myself a wedgie or having too much of my butt hang out.

I try to give myself a good look in the mirror, looking up and down. That isn't too hard because of how short my shorts are, but that also means that I don't look very pre-sentable. In Pennyworth the police would've been after me, maybe catcalling, or I would've been jumped on the way to the coffee shop. The fact that I haven't been, even here, still feels like an anomaly. Not only am I a teenage girl, but I'm a teenage girl that's out and about late at night by herself. And, forget the blogs that tell you not to leave the house unless your phone's above 80%, I don't even have a cell phone to use in case of emergency. That's less than 0%.

When I walk out, I give the barista my best look at being confident. She hands me my drink tenderly, and then she talks to me.

"Hey, are you okay? It's the middle of the night and you kinda walked here disheveled looking."

"I, uhh." I stammer to respond, "I could be better." With a nervous half chuckle, I manage to say, "My best friend is in the hospital. I tried to stay the night, but he snores a lot. I guess I just needed a break."

"You're free to hang out here if you'd like. My shift ends in another fifteen minutes, and I can give you a ride back to the hospital if you'd like. Or we can talk."

"Oh, I'd hate to take up your time. I'm sure you're exhausted, and you have places to go. You don't need to hear anything about what I've got going on."

"No, don't worry about it. I was gonna be out late, but my friends canceled plans this afternoon. And tomorrow's Saturday anyway. I'd rather you be safe than walking around by yourself."

"Is it really that dangerous here? In Pennyworth I would've been picked off the street by now. I figured it was safer because no one was around. No police patrol. No one mugged me. Even when I was dressed like this!"

"I think you're really lucky. I'm so glad that you didn't get hurt! Even if this isn't Pennyworth, I'd rather you not go out and about by yourself. Too many of my friends have made that mistake and gotten scared shitless. I've run home a couple of times just because some guys have picked up the pace as soon as they saw me. Maybe they wanted to offer me a ride home, but I decided not to take the risk. Luckily I was close to home."

"Oh, really? Gosh, I'm sorry! It sounds like it happens everywhere!"

"Of course it does, unfortunately. It's pretty kinda every-where. An English-ier word might be ubiquitous? I changed into my work uniform when I got here, so I have some extra stuff in the break room. Would you want a change of clothes? It'd probably fit you."

"I'd hate to do that to you."

"Please, don't worry about it. I'm happy to help you out!"

She hurries into what must be the break room, and I let the breath I've been holding in come out. Why have I been nervous around her? Or is it just because it's late and I don't want Blue to worry? Should I have found some way to contact my mom? I wonder if she's tried calling Blue and he wasn't able to answer. I guess I'll take a peek at his cell phone when I get back.

I finally take my first sip of the hot chocolate. It's very sweet, but good. It's also too hot, so I take the lid off. I look at the menu again, just for the sake of thinking about something besides the hospital. I still don't see black coffee on the menu, but I do see that they offer soymilk, coconut milk, and almond milk as alternatives. I've had hot chocolate with almond milk before. I wish I had seen it before I ordered. The almond milk makes it richer, and maybe it'd remind me a little bit more of home. Leave it to my mom to fulfill the Asian stereotype and be lactose intolerant–I haven't had dairy milk in years.

The pretty blonde comes out of the break room within five minutes, but she still says, "Sorry I took so long to get back to you. I guess my boyfriend left a few messages and got freaked when I didn't respond. Here are the clothes though."

For some reason, my heart drops. She has a boyfriend? Not that it matters "Can I at least give you some money for the clothes? I feel so badly." I look down at the cute purple flowy top and skinny jeans. They're both cuter than anything I've gotten from Jen's hand me downs. They even look like they might fit me.

"Don't worry about it!" She looks down at my cup of hot chocolate. "You haven't really touched your hot chocolate. Normally I'd down it!" She seems to contemplate something. "If you're really intent on paying me, just give me your hot cocoa. I'll make you something else that you'll like better. It's my fault that you didn't like it."

"Wait that's not paying you! I'd still be getting a drink! And really, it's fine. It tastes good, I guess I'm just used to almond milk."

"I'll make a new one with almond milk for you," she tells me, with a genuine smile this time. "If you want, you can even pay for it and we'll be even, okay?" She looks like she means it, and if I try to push any more that might be overdoing it. "I never got your name, by the way. I'm Sadie. Sadie Clifford. I'm from Pennyworth too."

"I'm Lacey, Lacey Matthews. I'm in my senior year. I'm surprised we haven't run into each other around school or anything before."

"My little sister is in school with you, and she's a senior. Do you know a Rosalyn?"

"I don't think so, no. But I should keep an eye out for her at the diner or something. What does she look like?"

"People say she looks a little like me. She's just a couple inches shorter, has some freckles and red hair. I think she's really pretty."

"I'll look out for her. If she's as nice as you are, well I hope that we can all be friends. Thank you so much for helping me, Sadie."

"Go ahead and get changed in the bathroom. I'll make this new hot chocolate for you." She ushers me as she heads behind the barista counter. Before I pass the counter, I dig into my pocket and grab another five and put it in front of her. It's more than the drink is worth, but I motion for her to keep it all.

When I go into the bathroom again, I take a second look at myself in the mirror. With a little laughter on my cheeks, I look less tired and even a little happier than I did twenty minutes ago. Apparently, not everyone in Pennyworth is a bitch, it's just that we're not allowed to be emotional there. There, being vulnerable about anything would've resulted in being told to "shut up, chin up."

I hurriedly get dressed, putting the pants on first. They're a little loose in the waist region, but they fit well over my wide hips. I look at myself in the mirror contentedly, in a bra and jeans, and I realize that my body is kind of…nice? The pale blue of the bra strap makes my skin look warm, and these are the best fitting jeans I've ever had. Before admiring myself for too long, I slip the purple top over my head. The sleeves would be kind of long if it were summer, but because it's nighttime in the spring, they're really comfortable. Before I go back outside, I attempt to flatten my hair out again. There really isn't any hiding bed head without a hairbrush, but I can at least try. I comb the hair through with my fingers again, and this time I moisten them with water. When I'm finally satisfied, I admire my work in the mirror. I feel more presentable and less embarrassed now.

When I walk back outside, I find Sadie sitting at our table with the two drinks and a couple of dollars' worth of change. Despite me not wanting it, she attempts to shove it into my hands before telling me that I look good in the clothes she's given me. When I reject it again, her face tells me that she's given up on trying to be much more charitable to me. And when I thank her for the clothes, tell her that I feel really good in them, her smile is back. The genuine one. And she's lovely.

We sit and talk for a little bit. No new customers come in, oddly enough, until after the guy taking over comes in for his shift to start and for Sadie's shift to end. And even after that is over, we talk for what must be another thirty minutes before we walk out to her car and she drives me to the hospital. We talk about Pennyworth, the teachers at school, the diner, how racist Mayor Jeffrey Wheaton is. We talk about how she knows that she's in a place of power because she's white, that her family is automatically safer because of the part of Pennyworth she lives in and because the police leave white people alone more than they should. And we talk about both of us living without a dad.

We both knew our dads, which is different. Most of the time dads just don't stick around long enough to see their kids born and see the damage they've left behind. SO maybe we're kinda special. I talk about the mysterious and popular John Matthews, and she tells me about the illustrious Jackson Clifford, about how her mom kept the last name when her parents divorced. She recognized my dad's name for some reason but couldn't pin it. I just chalked it up to him being so well known.

We both talk about how other men popped up in our lives, men that our moms dated short-term and hoped would be long-term father figures, men that–when they gave up on that sentiment–our moms dated because they were sad and in pain. I talk about my dad disappearing because of his death in a colored neighborhood. Sadie tells me about her father hitting her mom and yelling at everyone in the house, how he hit Rosalyn just once and that was what made her mom finally break and kick him out of the house. She told me about how she filed for divorce the next morning.

The ride to the hospital is nearly silent. I think we're both afraid that we overshared in the coffee shop. But could we have? In Pennyworth, you know that everyone around you has dealt with something as tragic as you have. The police are always suspect of everything that we do, and they're so quick to hold things against us, that it's become a huge cultural norm to just shut up about everything negative. To complain is to be ratted out. To be ratted out is to get gunshots early in the morning.

But outside of Pennyworth, when we didn't have to hide the emotional truth anymore, you get to know some of what that actually is.

Brigham knows how I have it tough living without my dad, but he doesn't know the full extent of it. He doesn't know that my mom and I got thrown apart from each other when it came to closeness. He doesn't know that I feel alone in my own home. He doesn't know that I miss Jen when she's away at college, that I fear the prospect of her never coming back to share a room with me. And what do I know about him?

Well, now I know that everything was enough for him to want to die. I know that he takes care of himself without the help of his parents. But he doesn't talk about what his parents are doing besides. He doesn't talk about how his parents separated. He doesn't talk about what his dad does at home, or what his dad's job is. I've never even been to his house, and I've kind of just taken it as a sign of respect to Brigham that I don't ask why.

When we stop in the hospital parking lot, Sadie doesn't just drop me off. She parks and follows me inside. And when I thank her for walking me in, the conversation goes something like: "Of course! But I'm also here to pick up my mom. I texted her telling her I was staying at work late, and I offered to pick her up and take her home so that she wouldn't have to take the bus into Pennyworth."

"Oh! That's nice of you. What department does she work in?"

"She works in the psychology facility, actually."

"Really? I know I didn't tell you why my friend was in the hospital, but he's actually staying in the psychology facility. What's your mom's name? Maybe she worked with him."

And before she answers, I hear a familiar voice come up from behind me. When I turn around to face the front desk, I see Gracie waving at the two of us. She happens to be leading Brigham by his arm, who's giving me a relieved smile.

"Hi, Sadie dear. And hi, Miss Matthews. I see you've met my daughter! I was just going to take Mr. Mathis back to his room. He was worried when he woke up and you were gone, so I said I'd sit out here with him for a little while to wait for you. You've come just in time." She directs the last part at me, and she lets out a gentle giggle. She reaches out her free arm to her daughter, and the two hug each other.

"Lacey, this is my mom, Gracie. I guess you two have already met."

"Nice to meet you again, Ms. Clifford. Thank you for taking care of Brigham for me. I hope I wasn't too long."

"Not at all," she smiles at me.

Suddenly Blue envelopes me in a hug. His patient gown crinkles between us, and I can feel him tremble a little. Gracie gently lets go of his arm and gives the two of us space, letting him kiss me on the forehead and wrap me up tightly with both arms. He doesn't say anything until we say goodbye to Gracie and Sadie.

At this point, he tells me, "I was worried when you left. Gracie told me that you left a note and that you'd be back really soon. I woke up like an hour ago to an empty room. I kinda freaked, I know…"

He trails off a little as he squeezes me a little tighter. In a moment we let go of the hug, and nurse Shelley walks up to us and offers to escort us back to the room. And at this point, Blue won't let go of my arm. When we get back to the room, he insists on pushing my air mattress closer to his bed before we go to sleep. By this point, it's almost five o'clock in the morning, and there's a little light coming through the window. He falls asleep again almost immediately–I can tell by the change in his breathing–but I stay up for almost another half hour, staring up at the hospital ceiling.

What happens after we go back to Pennyworth tomorrow? Is the emotion gone? Will I run into Sadie or Gracie again? Will I meet Rosalyn? Will Blue see the one shitty therapist in town? What changes now that I know what he's been hiding for at least six months?

CHAPTER 4

RETURN

———

The next morning, while Brigham is getting interviewed by a psychiatrist, I use his cell phone to call my mom and tell her that I'm fine. I tell her what's happened (with Brigham's permission) and she chokes out of surprise. Apparently, she'd only just gotten home from her boyfriend's, whatever his name is, apartment. I attempt not to act surprised and vaguely remember the erasable marker note that she left on the bathroom mirror. An even more distant memory is the name of this guy. Something that occurs to me much more clearly, is that her going out all the time with a guy (which she still hasn't introduced me to) has made it exceedingly easy for me to sneak out of the house to go on excursions with Blue. If only I'd taken advantage and actually gone out of the house more than once or twice a month. If I had never called her, would she have simply supposed that I left the house early for some reason unbeknownst to her?

When we check out of the hospital, we leave with the information that it would be best if Brigham went to therapy twice a week for at least the next six months and that he would need to take an antidepressant. The two of these, combined, would take up more than half of his weekly salary from the diner. And, of course, he'd already gotten into the habit of spending all of his money on what he needs week to week. He takes care of himself, and he even pays for his dad's drinking habit directly. If Blue pays for therapy, will he have enough to eat and pay the bills? Without his dad noticing? Fat chance.

He's told me before that he puts away what he can, that he's hoping to use the money he saves to go to community college at the same time that I start. The community college in the next town over is, quite luckily for the two of us, not very expensive. And the diner has already promised Blue that he has a place to work for as long as he needs. If he spends the money he's saved up carefully enough, he might have enough to pay for the first semester and textbooks at community. By the time the first semester is over, the six months of therapy will be done with and the dosage he takes the antidepressants might go down.

Even though this all ran through my mind as we were both updated, he explained that he'd rather just try therapy in the area and only add antidepressants if absolutely necessary. He told the nurse (which neither of us had seen before) that he wanted to be "normal" and that he didn't want to pump chemicals into his body if he didn't have to.

She started to tell us, "The antidepressants would give balance to the chemicals that are off balance and it's not just in his--"

He tells her, "It doesn't matter. I'll be back in town for therapy once I find a therapist I wanna try."

And then she gives in and agrees to let us out. She's probably just relieved that he's agreed to part of the prescribed treatment. And I know that I am, but I know well enough that he'll be able to afford community college if he's careful with his money. Is he just too proud to do as he's told? Does he think that anyone will look at him oddly for taking meds but that it'll be less weird if he goes to therapy? I know that I wouldn't, and with the way that Pennyworth works on an emotional level it's unlikely that anyone else would judge him or ever even know about him being depressed.

We're also told that his bicycle has been, ever so kindly, parked in a bike rack just outside the front doors of the hospital. Was this just a kind gesture of an EMT? Did I remember anyone grabbing his bicycle and ramming it into the back of the ambulance? I don't think so, but then again it was all a blur of *oh my god I hope he's still alive.*

When we finally get outside, he lets out a sigh of relief, as if he was escaping some sort of prison scenario. He's wearing the same clothes that he was wearing yesterday, just sans blood stains (apparently, they'd been washed pretty well by the hospital). And for a moment I remember yesterday before the blood was even on his clothes. The letterman jacket makes his shoulders look broader than usual, and he's puffing out his chest a little more than he typically would. But, of course, there's still the scabbing on the back of his head.

I see the bike rack and his old bike in the corner of my eye. There are a few more scratches than there normally are, but it's largely unchanged. If I hadn't just ridden it yesterday, it would've looked like Brigham was on one of his personal excursions around Pennyworth. Maybe he fell on the way to the liquor store when he was getting his dad's booze. Maybe he dropped it when he reached my front yard. No one would suspect anything out of the blue. I grab the bike from the bike rack and walk it the two feet over to Brigham, and he takes the handlebars from me. I half expect him to mount and offer me the handlebars, but instead he just starts walking and uses his head to tell me to follow.

"Where are we going?"

He responds, "I don't really know, but I don't think that I'm quite ready to head back home. Did you find any quiet places last night? Any sights we should see before we go back?"

"Not really, I just went to the coffee shop where I met Sadie, who I guess is Gracie's daughter coincidentally? We just talked for a while. I think I just needed to get out of my own head for a little bit last night."

"At this hour it's probably busy as fuck there. Maybe we can go somewhere else? How'd the call with your mom go?"

"It went alright, I think. For a second she almost reacted and had a little emotion, but, of course, she choked it back before I could hear her cry. She was mostly just surprised to hear about it, I guess. She's glad you're okay though, really glad. She could never tell you to your face, but I can tell she's glad you're around."

"Hah, why? So she doesn't have to deal with you all the time?"

"Heh, maybe. Or maybe she's just glad that I actually have a friend to drag me out of the house every once in a while. Before I met you, well we both know that I didn't go out much unless I was with my dad. Once he died, I really needed someone to be around somehow. I think she thinks that she wouldn't have made the cut."

"Your mom doesn't know what she's made of, does she? She works all the time so that Jen doesn't have to worry about working through college and so that she can take care of you. And she does it by herself. Sure, Ms. Wong could be at home a little more, but she's doing her best y'know?"

"I guess I do. She's just doing her best to move on past my dad and take care of her daughters. Sometimes I wish that we were closer, but Pennyworth doesn't really warrant that. She smiles and hugs me most of the time when I come home from school. She always leaves snacks for me in the fridge. She makes sure the house is quiet when I'm working on school stuff, which is most of the time. And because of that, well I'm sure she can't help being out of the house at least sometimes. I'm glad that she's trying to make sure that she's happy too. I mean, she's a teacher at the elementary school, and she works shifts at the Ready-Mart whenever she can get them. I'm just relieved that she's found someone she thinks is worth her time."

"Yeah. She certainly does more than my dad. I know I haven't talked about it a whole lot before, but that douche is a raging alcoholic. I don't know if he's ever sober long enough to remember that Donte died."

"I feel like that really isn't fair, that you have to take care of yourself and mourn that on your own. God, is that really possible? Not that there's much space in Pennyworth to deal with that anyway. If you start crying in public, people immediately leave or tell you to keep your chin up. One of those or they just get really pissy."

"Not like I can do much at home either. My dad used to hit me when he found me in my bedroom crying. At least he was sober enough to care about me some of the time then. I would take the meds the hospital just prescribed, but he makes me add money to his booze fund. I can't afford to actually buy the damn meds. If I did both the therapy and the meds, I wouldn't be able to afford community college. And, with therapy, there's no way I'll be able to think about getting an apartment away from him until the second semester. When the tap dries up, maybe he'll finally have an 'oh-shit' moment and get it in his head how shit he is."

At this point, we've stumbled upon a park. This one is nothing like the one in Pennyworth-- the trees and the grass are too well-kept and the benches actually exist-- and we decide to sit down. He sits down first, and I rest my head on his chest. I reach up and run my fingers over and through his hair for a few minutes. When I garner the courage, I ask him, "So what now? What changes?"

"Nothing, if we can manage it. On Monday I go to work and you go to school. Today and tomorrow you do your homework and I try to get you to follow me to the diner or around town because I know community college won't care how well you're doing in your classes. I keep hiding this shit from everyone like I've been doing since November. The only thing that's changed is that now you and Ms. Wong know what's up, that I'm going to the library at some point to find therapists that I can afford, and that I have to plan on being alive for longer than another negative twenty-one hours."

He says the last part like he's trying to be funny, and I nervously laugh at the realness of it all. "Do you want to be alive right now?" I have to ask him.

"Kinda. I mean you're here. I kinda am still afraid that I'm gonna get in the way of your success. But, I kinda figured out that it wouldn't do anyone any good if I was dead like Donte."

Him saying that last bit about Donte catches me a little bit off guard. "I kinda thought something like that in the hospital last night. Y'know how you felt betrayed by Donte when he died, even though you knew it wouldn't be his fault?" I pause when he nods in slow understanding. "I thought about that and realized that I would've felt betrayed by you if you left me alone. I mean, I lost my dad, my sister's off at college, and my mom is only around so much. I would've lost my best friend too."

I start to tear up a little bit at the fresh thought of losing Blue. But he kisses my forehead as if to tell me that he understands what I mean. That's what this kiss means. He means *I get it*. At least I think that's what it means.

And then he tells me, "I'm not leaving you."

We stay there until it's four o'clock and decide it's time to go back home. Not that we want to go back, but we'll be hungry for dinner soon enough and the diner churns out a bunch of fresh food right when they open at five thirty. Not that it tastes amazing when it's fresh, but it's definitely its greasiest and least soggy when it's that way.

After talking about the future, after crying for a while, and after enough discussion and remembrance of the past, we muster up the strength to stand up and take the bike back home. When he offers me his handlebars, I remember the pros and cons of wearing shorts instead of jeans on his bike.

While the metal is less hot against jeans, jeans are simultaneously sweatier and more slippery than shorts are. Of course, not sticking to the handlebars also meant less friction, so it was significantly less painful to just wear jeans. The pain that comes with wearing shorts on his handlebars is so significant, it almost makes having to adjust when I slide around wearing jeans feel like nothing.

Regardless of the circumstances-- the depression and the hospital and the least important change in clothes-- we still managed to do the normal things on the way home.

At first, we rode home kinda solemnly. It was clear we didn't know what else we were allowed to say, almost like we didn't know what to say as we switched from resting in a place where emotion was safe, to traveling back to where emotion was a secret. Were we in the place of secrecy yet? Certainly not, but what else was there to say? One thing, maybe.

"What did you and Donte used to do together?"

"When we were really young, we'd do the normal brother stuff. We'd fight over toys, we'd dig holes in the backyard, we'd try to sneak out of the house when our parents weren't looking. I remember that when our parents would fight and we could hear them yelling in the living room, I would always sneak over to his side of our room and try and sleep with him in his bed. Whenever I tried to do it otherwise, he would push me away and tell me to go back to bed, but he made an exception when mama and my dad would fight with each other. He just knew what I needed, I guess. He always seemed to know what I needed a little bit better than I did. And when my mom left, he got really quiet. I could tell that he missed her. The two of us kinda started to drift apart when she was gone. We'd try and keep tabs on each other, but he had a job and I had school. And when I quit school to get a job, suddenly we were both almost never home."

It's so odd. He's talking about his mom like she's dead, too. "Heh, I'm glad you had that. Jen would never let me share her bed with her. Before she went to school, do you remember? she had a curtain put up in the center of the room as a partition so that I wouldn't be able to go over to her side of the room as easily. I guess mom and my dad didn't fight much in the house, and they both loved me so much that they couldn't have thought about fighting in front of me. My dad even loved Jen like she was his own, even though she looked nothing like him and more like our mom."

"I think it's good that he loved you guys so much, and it's so obvious that your guy's mom loves you so much now. Your dad must've stuck around a lot longer than hers, considering when your dad got into the picture."

"It's true. I never met her father, and my dad was around for over eight years. She probably misses him sometimes. I wonder if that's why she never wanted to be close to me. Sure, we had the same mom, but I think she thought we were too different to ever like each other much. She actually told me once, 'Stop trying to be close to me. We aren't the same blood and I wouldn't be friends with you if I met you outside of family'. I didn't know that she felt that way until after my dad died, and now she's in college. She really didn't want it, so the house doesn't feel that different. It's about as empty, and I actually have more space in my room since the partition isn't up in there anymore." *How much of that is true?*

After I say that, Blue is quiet for a while, so I keep talking. "But I'm really glad that you and Donte had each other for a while. You needed him and you were close, even though your parents didn't want to be."

"Yeah, I'm really lucky on that front. It still stings like hell that he's gone, that my mom cheated on my dad and got kicked out of the house. But I had him, and I have you still, and your mom cares about me way more than mine ever could have. All in all, I think I wound up okay, despite all of the circumstances that made that nearly impossible for me. It's funny though. Your mom somehow shows how much she cares about you without saying anything outright. She doesn't say she loves you, but she always keeps the house quiet when you need it, and she cooks for you, and she works so hard."

"It sucks, huh? Feeling like your parents don't love you. But that's crazy to me, just because I love you so much. I couldn't ever picture someone not caring about you once they get to know you."

"My dad used to love me. He used to cook all the time and would take Donte and I on walks around the neighborhood and give us piggyback rides. He always helped me with homework in elementary school. And then, when my mom got kicked out, he just changed. It was like a switch flipped inside of him. He started drinking all the time, and Donte and I were just working all the time."

"Y'know, I didn't know this much about you until we finally got out of Pennyworth together. I'm not really outside of town much. I didn't know your mom cheated on your dad. I didn't know that you felt like that about my mom. I didn't know that you would run to your brother when your parents fought before. It's so different to actually know something about you."

"I know. It's almost the same for you. I wouldn't have ever known that about you and Jen. It's almost like, in Pennyworth, you can tell that everyone is hiding something, you can almost tell what it is, but never just quite well enough. And I think everything would change and be better if everyone would stop being too proud to say something. We all know that no one in this town is one-hundred-percent okay. But we don't know our neighbors or the kids at school or," I hear him take a deep sigh, "or even our best friends."

I'm surprised that he's right, that he knows just as little about me as I know about him. "Hey, but we know a little bit better now. And I think that's a good start." I let out an audible sigh, like one of simultaneous relief and joy. "Maybe we can do something about it."

And without answering me, suddenly Blue picks up speed. Before I know what he's doing, I feel butterflies in my stomach as we launch off of the ground and up into the air. And on the way up and down and for I don't know how long, he starts giving one of those *Dead Poets Society* screams. And it's right in my ear so I almost feel it coming before it does. When we've finally landed, I start to let out a "YAAAW-WWP" of my own, and we laugh about it, like it's an homage to all of the change we've just created in ourselves. Like 'hey, look, it's still me. I know we just told each other all of this ugly stuff, but, fuck it, I still think you're great and hilarious and the best friend I've ever had.'

Still, even with the comfort of long-held memories, my heart aches a little bit. I don't even know the name of the town I'm leaving, and this is the freest I've been in years. Whether it's worrying about Brigham being shot at by the police just because he's black, or whether it's my being afraid of being called a chink wherever I go, or just facing a place where I know I won't be able to cry in front of the people I love without the fear of being scolded. I don't know if this town is special or if Pennyworth is especially fucked up, but returning is going to definitely be difficult.

Then again, Gracie and Sadie have agreed to see me at the diner at some point. Before we left the hospital, Gracie put both of their numbers into Brigham's cell phone. Maybe we'll all be able to get together, and maybe we'll get to have a little bubble of honesty, where we can say what we mean. Where the incessant scolding to keep your chin up and stop your crying isn't integral to our interaction. I wonder if Rosalyn is the same.

When we get past the wall cross into the town limits (after lots of convincing the cops that the hospital papers were real) we pass one of those cheesy sign that says "Welcome to Pennyworth: Keep your chin up! -Mayor Jeffrey Wheaton." I don't know when the mayor coined that, or when he thinks he came up with that, but the saying has been on that sign for long enough for the sign to have experienced some significant wear. It was there when I was in elementary school. I remember going to the sign after school all the time, waiting to see if the words would change. It was the only way I could think of that might tell me when Jeffrey Wheaton wasn't mayor anymore.

When I was that little, I didn't even care that much about him because I didn't know what being mayor really meant. I didn't know that he was actively encouraging the racist tendencies of the police force or that he was withholding funding for the schools or that he refused to let books and information be updated in the library. I didn't know those things until I heard my parents complaining about it enough. My mom being in the school system really gives her a lot of inside information on that stuff. And I'm guessing my dad knew so much because he knows everyone and talks to everyone. I heard them sit at the kitchen table and just complain about the fact that there was so much maltreatment, especially in our own neighborhood.

And the sign just never changed. I could never explain why he kept getting re-elected, why he'll probably get reelected next term. The support for him definitely doesn't exist in my neighborhood, but it's probable that the white neighborhoods outnumber the ones with people of color. If it's not that (and that's possible because democracy has been so fucked) I wouldn't be surprised if he somehow had it rigged.

Did Pennyworth not used to be so emotionally empty? Did that change with the mayor? My mom might know. Gracie would probably know too.

We arrive at the diner quickly after crossing through the town border. And once we get to the front door, Brigham holds up his phone to me and shows me the time: 5:34. Underneath is a picture of the two of us: a selfie with a sunset in the background from the last time we went to the beach.

"Hey, Blue," I say, causing him to look up at me, "Do you wanna just pick up and head to the beach? We can watch the sunset and stuff."

"That'd be fun," he smiles at me, "but we'd better be careful to not get your new clothes wet."

"Eh, I'll just roll up my sleeves and cuff the jeans a little. We can just wade if that's alright with you."

"Yeah, but that's what you say all the time. You say that we'll just wade but wind up pushing me in, or you bother me until I put you in a headlock and pull you in." He laughs at the prospect of the memories.

"Would that be so bad though? Clothes can be washed, and we always wind up having a good time, don't we? Don't be such a wet blanket!" I laugh out the last sentence.

"Well, I won't be if you don't push me in!" He laughs the pun back at me. "Come on let's get in there before the fries aren't fresh anymore." And he pushes himself into the familiar restaurant.

There are torn blue leather stools in front of the serving counter, there's black and white tiling on the floor, and there are cushy booths with the same color seating as the stools. The jukebox is piping Queen through the restaurant, and the restaurant is pretty empty. But that's normal for opening time. No one really rushes here for food, especially since it's kinda the only fast food fare in town and the menu isn't exactly huge. I've had everything on the menu at least four times, and I've come to learn that the best things are the fries, the milkshakes, and the double cheeseburgers.

Some people tell me over and over that the bacon cheeseburgers are better, but I've never been a bacon person. Maybe it's just because the only bacon I've ever had is at the diner and like once at home, but the one at the diner is way too greasy, and the way that my dad made it was limp and weird.

While Blue is ordering for the two of us from one of the guys behind the register, I ask a second person behind the counter if the diner is accepting applications for work. He hands me a single sheet of paper with a questionnaire about availability and work ethic, as well as a spot for an ID number. "I don't have an ID, just one for school. Is that alright?"

"Sure, just make sure that you get a work permit from the school and specify that your ID number is for a school ID. You'll have a casual interview immediately after you return the application with the permit. For students, typically, as long as you have a 2.0 GPA, we'll take you. But I don't suspect that'll be a problem for you, aha."

I know he's talking about the fact that I'm Asian, but I play dumb anyway, "What do you mean I won't have a problem? Do I know you?"

He kinda fidgets before he answers, "No, no it's cuz you're a chink. Aren't all you guys smart?"

"Hmm, I don't know if that's true, but I certainly am." Something that I've learned over the last little while, is that guys get pissed if you agree with any compliments that they give you. And, especially because this guy is all about perpetuating stereotypes, I didn't think it was quite a shame to make him visibly bothered.

"Hey, I bet you're not even that smart! You're not all that!"

"You're the one that said all Asians are smart. Sounds like you're contradicting yourself. Next thing you know you'll tell me I'm pretty; I'll tell you I'm well aware and that information is ubiquitous, and then you'll throw a pissy fit at me for agreeing with you a second time."

"Hah! As if! Shut up ya chink! You wish I thought you were cute!"

"Well, now I never said anything about my being cute, but you're not wrong about that either. Hm." I pivot away from the counter, holding my application as if it were a designer handbag or some other sort of thing that symbolizes power. That's what movies do right? The popular girls flash their designer bags to make some poor protagonist feel shitty about herself.

He sounds like he wants to stay something in response but is too frustrated to do more than grunt and bite his tongue. And at this point, I walk toward the entrance of the diner to where Brigham is waiting with our food. I can tell from the wide smile on his face that he's well aware of what just went down between me and the poor sap of a cashier. The first couple of times that stuff like that happened to me he would jump in to rescue me, but he quickly realized that I didn't need it all that much. There's only been one time where the person picking on me got so intense that Brigham had to step in and scare them off. There was this big stocky guy that was trying to push me up against the wall when I went to the restroom, and when I tried to shove him off Brigham overheard what was going on. I think the only thing that scared him off was that he saw a black guy coming his way. And he said, out loud, "Sorry man, I didn't mean to hit on a dude's chick like that." And I'm glad that Blue was able to step in, but why does it work that way? Can't I just be respected whether I'm dating a guy or not? I'm all at once bothered at the thought of dating my best friend and thankful that we were perceived to be dating.

Since that happened, I'm positive that Blue likes to stick around at least a little bit because he feels like he can protect me every once in a while. Maybe he forgot that stuff when he wrote his suicide note, or maybe he thinks that I don't need help because most of the time I'm able to handle shit on my own. When did that happen anyway? A year ago? A little less? Definitely before Donte got shot. Have I been too independent since then? Is that a thing that's possible? We both walk out of the diner listening to Freddie Mercury telling us "Driving back in style, in my saloon will do quite nicely… Just take me back to yours that will be fine…"

We get to the beach in record time. The entire way here, it feels like Brigham pedals harder than usual. At first, I worry that he just wanted to get out of the diner because he was so pissed, but a first look at his face after I dismount his handlebars tells me that he's actually just excited to be out of the main bit of town. We're not out of Pennyworth, but we're pretty far away from most of the people. It's the middle of spring, so almost no one is here. Just in case anyone ever wondered, the beach is still pretty fucking great in the spring. The sand doesn't get too sticky, even though it's still really course. Some of the bushes have little flowers blossom, and the ocean blazes this amazing bright blue! The water isn't as warm as it would be in the winter, but that's okay. And on the cloudless days, oh my god on the cloudless days, the sky looks gigantic.

I take the handlebars from him and bring the bike down the paved pathway that leads down to the sand, and he walks behind me with the food in one hand and his other hand in a Letterman pocket. We're mostly quiet on the way down to the beach, and we were actually pretty quiet on the way from the diner. But it's not a sad quiet, like it's been for the last twenty-four hours. He's happy right now. And I can tell that the air is different than when it was weeks ago, before the suicide attempt. It's even different from last November first, the morning where Blue learned that Donte had died.

He's not all the way better, and his emotions aren't fixed. But, then again, his emotions aren't a machine. Even his next few actions tell me that he feels more hopeful. He tries to steal the bike from me to run ahead of me, but then I swerve it out of the way. He goes with it and jogs in front of me for a little bit, daring me to catch up with him. He laughs and waves the brown bag of food out in front of him, knowing full well I'll chase after him for food almost without exception.

So I throw the bike down onto the sidewalk and plow full speed ahead at him. We've made it to the part of the beach where the sand sinks a little when you step on it, so I don't worry much about pushing him over. At the last moment, I duck down and grab his legs, making him land ass first into the sand and then causing him to fall all the way back. As I scramble up to the bag he holds above the top of his head, his other hand goes to my stomach.

"Ahhh! Hahahaha! Hah... ha... Hah. Brigham! Stop it!" While he tickles me, I clutch the greasy bag close to my body and roll onto the sand next to him. It's in this position that he lies still. And then I lie still. We stay that way for a while. After a moment or two, I finally reach into the bag to grab my double cheeseburger and take a large bite. Like I said earlier, the food isn't amazing, but it's best when it's fresh. The grease, at the very least, is kinda addicting.

As I chew, Blue looks over at me with disbelief and says, "Oh my god, Lacey. I will never believe that you eat like that! You're gonna kill yourself if you keep taking big ass bites like that." He says it all with amused undertones, so I know that the irony isn't lost on him.

"Buh ahm sho huugrie" I respond will a full mouth. When I finally swallow, I manage to say, "The food at the hospital sucks and you know it!" At this statement, my appendages go outward, and I sprawl into a starfish. I know that the motion makes it look like I'm making a big deal about something important. "And besides, why wouldn't you be eating too?" I take another humongous bite before letting him respond.

"Come on, the food wasn't even that bad," he chuckles. He grabs his bacon cheeseburger (ick.) and makes a grand gesture out of taking a slightly smaller than normal sized bite, as if to show me how gentlemen and fancy people eat. Out of protest, I take an even bigger bite than the last one. "By the way, why'd you grab an application? You know that your mom's already going to offer to put you through college, and Jen would probably help out too."

I have to chew fast and take a big gulp of beef that kinda hurts my throat to swallow before I can answer. "I know that they'll help me out, but it's mostly for you. I'd rather you get out of the house and find a way to stay in an apartment during your first semester. And you don't even have to feel badly about it cuz I'll be your roommate. I'd be paying half the rent, so it wouldn't even be charity!"

"Lacey, that's not how it works. I'd have to sleep on the couch, idiot." With the last word, he sits up and laughs while ruffling my hair.

In the middle of the hair ruffling, I sit up to be on his level. "We could take turns on the couch, or we could get one of those couches that folds out into a bed, or we could share a room. I wouldn't care too much. Hell, let me take the couch."

He opens his mouth to stop me, but I interrupt him.

"Come on, Blue. I want you to feel stable about this whole therapy thing. And I would love to live with you during college. I'd do almost anything to not be away from my best friend, and you know you'd do the same thing for me if I were in your situation! I bet you'd try to be even nicer and just straight up pay for the apartment without offering to live with me, but I'm nice. This way you don't have to feel bad, AND you won't be lonely." I give him a big smile.

He leans over to give me a kiss on the forehead. "Thank you, Lacey."

"Anything for you, Blue."

By the time that Brigham gets me home, it's after one in the morning. I try to sneak into the house quietly so that I don't wake my mom, but when I pass my mom's bedroom, I hear stifled sobs. There's no light coming from underneath the door, but I know that she's awake. I knock quietly and then push the door open, and when I walk in my mom is crying on her bed in the darkness, her face in the pillow and her arms are wrapped tightly around her torso. There's just enough moonlight flooding in through the window to make out the shape of her face and the silhouette of her body.

"Mama?" I walk in quickly and turn on the lamp on her bedside table. I jump into her bed and take her into my arms. "Mama, are you okay? What's going on?"

"I've been home. Lacey, it's alright. Nothing happened. Your call just scared me, and I haven't really been myself today. It's alright, okay?"

"Mama, I've never seen you cry like this. The last time I saw you cry this much was when Papa died, and that went on for weeks, and you'd barely talk about it with me or Jenny. You have to tell me what happened."

As I move closer to her, she chokes a little bit before she shakes her head.

"I know it's taboo out there, but we're home now. No one can get pissed at us here. And I know that you don't really like talking, but you have to talk at some point or else..."

"Or else, what?"

"I'm afraid that if you don't talk, you'll wind up like me. It comes up eventually y'know. I don't want you to wind up talking to strangers about stuff. Tell me. Tell me, Mama."

"It was just the call. You don't have a lot of friends and I didn't want you to lose Brigham. I know how much you care about him. If you lost him, I was afraid you wouldn't have anyone. Jenny is off at college and you'd really only have me. But I'm not a teenager. You either wouldn't talk to me or I might not understand everything the way that you'd want me to. That's how it worked with my mom and dad. And it was always so much easier for you to connect with your dad than it was for you to connect with me. He took you to the park and taught you and Jenny how to ride your bikes, and all I could manage to do in order to say I loved you three, was to cook and take a couple jobs. I don't know how to say those things, Lacey, and I've always felt so wrong about that."

"I know, Mama, but Brigham isn't gone. He's fine. He wanted to go to the diner and to the beach today. We rode on his bike and yelled like idiots and we went swimming even though we had to do it in our clothes. He's alive, Mama."

"Lacey, he almost wasn't. If he didn't have you there with him, he would have gotten to the bottom of the hotel the wrong way and you would've lost him. You were so close to losing him. You can't possibly act like all of this is normal, baby."

"I never said that it was," and now I can't help letting a couple tears stream down my face. "But he's alive and okay, and he felt better today because of me. He'll start therapy in a couple of weeks. And because we went to the hospital, I met someone who might be friends with me. Everything wound up just fine. That's how I got home…"

And I have to pause and take a breath before I can go on. "And I kinda feel like if I treat him like he's another person, like that absolutely everything has changed, that'll make him feel even worse about what's gone on. He's mostly the same once I get him moving. He's even letting me help him split rent when college starts, so I'm gonna work part time at the diner over the summer. Maybe sooner."

She kinda looks at me like she's in disbelief about the whole situation. But, can I really blame her? The most important person in her daughter's life was almost gone. This is the guy that she's treated as her son since the two of them had met. "Aren't you just aching to cry about all of this, though?"

This time I'm the one that chokes a little before I speak. "Mama, of course I am. But I feel like I've cried enough in the last thirty-six hours. I cried the entire time that I waited for visiting hours to start at the hospital. I cried when I slept at the hospital. I woke up in the middle of the night at the hospital and had to take a walk to calm down. I've been crying for hours, and it still feels like it hasn't been enough. Right now, I just wanna be relieved that he's still here, that he's still our Brigham Blue." Even in the middle of my saying this, I can't keep tears from rolling onto my cheeks and having to squeeze my stomach and lungs to get the words out all the way.

Honestly, I've been terrified all day that I'd lose him, even though he never insinuated that he wanted to die after we'd left the hospital. And I've been relieved every time that he reached out to touch me that I wasn't at the beach with a ghost. What if he's gone when I wake up tomorrow?

My mom and I spend a couple of hours in her bedroom, just lying there and mostly being quiet. Sometimes we'd say something to each other. "Hey, do you want some tea? Can I get you a snack? What if things had been different? What if... What if... What if...?" And, of course, neither of us were very hungry. And, of course, neither of us knew any of the answers for the what if questions.

What if my dad were alive?

What if he were here right now?

What if Brigham really were dead?

What if the two of us had never been friends?

What if we didn't live in Pennyworth and could actually speak without fear?

She has to fall asleep before I can justify getting up and trying to head to bed. And even before I go to sleep, I have to grab the landline and punch in Brigham's number. He answers in half a ring and I hear shuffling for several seconds before he speaks into the microphone. "Hey, Lace. I had a feeling you'd still be awake."

"Hey, Blue. Just making sure you got home alright, but I had to check on my mom for a little while before I could say anything."

"How's Ms. Wong? Is she okay? What's wrong?"

"She's just spooked about you. If you were gone, and I don't think she's exactly wrong either, she said that I wouldn't have anyone to depend on if I needed it. She was really scared about the whole thing. She was kinda surprised that you were up for hanging out so much tonight."

"Honestly, so am I. I think that a flipped kinda switched I started comparing me dying to my brother dying. I realized that I couldn't do that to you, at least not on purpose. I know that Donte didn't have any say in the matter..." he pauses for a small chuckle, "but I'm still hurt about it. Just think if he wanted to die and leave me, that shit would've hurt even worse than fucking hell."

"I'm glad that that meant that much to you. It really would suck if you left like that. Even if I could be the richest fucking person in the world with you gone, I'd never choose that. You mean a lot to me, Blue."

"You mean a lot to me too, Lace. Thank you for today. I'm really fucking glad that you were there for me yesterday. If you were gone--"

His sentence stops midway, and over the phone speaker, I hear a bang on the other side of the conversation. Blue doesn't even make much of a sound. I just hear his phone move a little bit when he jumps in reaction to the sound of a gunshot.

"Blue, are you okay? What happened?"

"Even though I'm like two steps from my house, one of the policemen gave a warning shot toward me for being out. I should go. Luckily," he lowers the register of his voice, "he's a really poor shot. It might as well have just been a firework going off cuz I didn't get hit."

I didn't know that he was outside. The police patrols his neighborhood like crazy, and they do it so randomly that you can't predict it. It's the police's fault that that's the part of town with the most fucked up looking streets. There are skid marks and cracks on the actual streets themselves. The houses have lots of patchwork drywall from having to patch up nicks and holes from bullets. That, in turn, makes the paint peel faster.

At least, in my neighborhood, there's fewer of everything. Almost no skid marks. I think that my house only has one or two drywall patches, max. It doesn't matter that he's only a handful of blocks away from me. It's just that much worse, and I wish I knew why.

"Go inside, Blue. Quick. I'll see you tomorrow. And I might as well pretend that was a firework, for my own peace of mind."

"I'm in the kitchen now. I'll pretend, too. Good night, Lacey. I love you."

"Good night, Blue. I love you too."

Before I go to bed, I hear a couple more fireworks go off in my neighborhood. And I flashback to my dad getting hit by a not firework, almost ten years ago. I hope that I don't hear any not-fireworks tonight.

CHAPTER 5

UP

It's been two weeks since Brigham has been discharged from the hospital and we've been spending as much time as we possibly can with each other. Luckily, senior year hasn't required hours and hours of work every night because he meets up with me immediately after school and brings me home no earlier than ten o'clock. And I know that my mom would ordinarily be worried about me staying out so late, just because that's who she is, but with the recent suicide attempt she treats it differently. If this had suddenly come out of nowhere, I would've been scolded, but this isn't two kids going out every night to get high or drunk or vandalize the non-existent cars of most of our neighbors.

This is predominantly going to the beach and to the diner. This is mostly talking to each other in private places where Pennyworth citizens won't tell us to keep our chins up or whatever the fuck. This is tickle fights and forehead kisses and bicycle rides and trying to find the name of the town with the hospital by scoping the border for signs with "Welcome to" written in big white chalky letters. Of course, the wall and the policemen make that a little harder, but we make do with the notches of the occasional chain-link fence and the shorter gates at entry points (from a distance, of course).

And we do all of this immediately after I get out of school. Brigham must've changed his work hours around after he tried to die, just so he could meet up with me right when school ends. And I can only imagine the things people imagine about us now that we're more visible to the public eye. It's not that people are surprised about us spending time with each other in general: we've been friends for years, so we aren't new to each other. But no one knows about the suicide attempt. And anyone who knows me is well aware of how I keep to myself at home with homework. Actually, people who don't know that about me might as well assume it because of the chink's lifestyle that's been stereotyped. Given that... Yikes. It looks like we're dating to the onlooking eye.

I couldn't ever do that. It's just that it's Brigham. He's been my best friend for years, and he's practically my brother with the way that my mom treats him and the way that we interact with each other. The friendship dynamic is something I can never see changing. It's lasted for so long...

"Lacey, are you listening to me?" He's offering his hand to me to indicate that we should get going. I must've gotten too distracted thinking about him almost being gone. I start to walk off on my own, though. Without grabbing his hand. "Woah, Lace, are you alright? What's up?"

"I don't need the whole school thinking I'm dating you, Blue."

"I don't think anyone gives two shits, okay? They've seen us walking around holding hands before. Girls have flirted with me WHILE we've been holding hands. People know this about us."

I sheepishly take his hand in mine as we walk down to the street. Brigham's right. No one thinks anything of us. At least, they don't think of us any differently today than they did when the two of us first met. But still. Are people looking at me differently?

I see a few people glance at me and then dive into conversations. It's hard to tell if the topics are old or if they've just now started. Is this what paranoia feels like? But Blue doesn't seem to care about what everyone is saying or how they're looking at us. Maybe because it's always been this way. Or maybe he just genuinely doesn't care about the prospect of people from his old high school spreading rumors.

"Lacey?" Blue's voice makes me jump. "I think you're still too much in your head about this, Lace. No one cares. It's okay. And even if they did, what's so wrong with people thinking that you have a life outside of homework?"

"Okay, okay. Sorry. You're right." I feel kinda brushed off and pissed off at this, but I try to hide it. "What are we up to today? Heading to the diner? The beach?"

"Maybe later, but I was kinda hoping that we could go back to the hotel. Visit it and kinda say, 'alright this is where I wanted shit to go badly, but something forced me to keep going on with something'. I mean, I'm not saying we pray or anything, but I kinda want closure or something, y'know?"

"Woah." My mood suddenly changes. "Are you sure? It's happened so recently. Are you gonna be alright about it?"

"I've been wanting to go back there for a little bit. The closure bit I feel like would be good for me. Maybe we could make it a place that isn't just a bad memory to us. We could just hang out there for a little bit and see how we feel about it."

"Okay, but if something's going on, I'll know about it. The only reason I'm letting you go is because you're letting me come along. This kinda sounds like you wanna have an excuse to go back there regularly without me worrying about you. If you fucking use this as an excuse to try and kill yourself again, I'm gonna kill you, Blue."

"Heh. Do you get the irony of that? Hah!"

"Blue... Is that what you're planning on?"

"I mean, it crossed my mind--"

"Blue! We can't fucking do that--!"

"--I mean it crossed my mind in the way that you think about jumping off a cliff even though you know that you won't. I'm not gonna kill myself, Lacey! In fact, I promise I won't ever go back to the rooftop without you."

"Swear on my life, Blue."

"Lacey, uh, don't you mean on my life?"

"No, I mean on mine. If you go to the rooftop without me, I'll be as good as dead to you. I don't care if you think about killing yourself or not. I don't give a fuck."

"Alright, alright. I swear."

I don't know how much I believe him.

We pull ourselves up to the second story relatively quickly. But when we make it up it occurs to me that all of the doors in the hotel are unlocked but we haven't used the front door. "Is there a reason we haven't tried to use the front door?"

"It's both stuck and made of metal. I tried pulling it open several times, but it just doesn't budge."

"Well, what about the windows on the first story? Couldn't we break one open? Or, what are the odds that we could push up and the locks would be too weak to hold it open?"

"Similar issue there, I guess. The wood's so warped and swollen it doesn't really go up. And, oddly enough, they're using bulletproof glass down there. The only way I could ever get up here was with the second story window. It was partially open already. I got lucky with this, I guess."

"Do you think we could go downstairs today and try the door from the inside? Or unlock one of the windows? It'd be a lot less than doing this."

"I don't know, Lace. I've wanted to and I almost tried it, but then I figured out that a couple of gangs want access to the rooftop, and the police wouldn't mind knowing about it either. If we loosen up anything, anyone might discover it and use it. I kinda like that right now it's nothing to everyone else. It's so quiet here. I like that."

I get kinda quiet at that. I guess it's always been pretty clear that Brigham and I are both introverted, so I shouldn't be too surprised. But how does he know about these gangs? And how hard are they really trying to get up here? I can see the appeal because it's a great place for storage and there's a major vantage point the higher up you go. Gangs with access to this place wouldn't even have to worry a lot about police patrol because no one lives out here and no one ever comes out here. Well, at least those things wouldn't be a problem at first. They might be issues eventually. I haven't even seen any squatters. "How do you know about this gang stuff? Are you trying to get into one?"

"No, no. Hell no. People from Nail have been talking about it at the diner, trying to be secretive about it. But they hush up when people from Wood come by. And they've been talking about how they hope that they'll get access to the rooftop too, even though they know that won't really be the case."

"How can you tell which people are from which?"

"Cuz Nail's the biggest white gang in Pennyworth. One might say they're getting ready to be the racist cops of tomorrow. They sure do act like them enough."

"I didn't know that the gangs were as racist as that. I thought it was enough that it was just the cops picking on the people in the colored parts of town. I mean, honestly, I don't know anything about either of the gangs."

"Well, anyway, I'd rather keep them from finding out about how to get up here. This is the only way I've found, and I'd like to keep it a secret that I even know about it. They'd tear me apart if they found out I knew anything."

"If they're as bad as you say they are, well I'd like to keep them as far away from here as possible. Have they ever seen you up here?"

"Not yet, but I guess that's because most of the time I'm here alone. Once I heard people walking by and I peered down and saw a group of them, but that's the closest encounter I've had with any of them outside of the diner. I just never know when they're coming, so I'm always afraid that they'll hear me or see me somehow."

It isn't long before we reach the top of the stairwell and are able to walk through the doorway that leads to the roof. By the time that we get there, the topic has morphed from talking about the gangs' potentials of finding us (Wood too) into actually talking about the roof and the attempt.

"The last time we were here, we were only here for like a couple hours."

"Hey, I already promised you that I wouldn't come back here without you. What else do I have to promise?" He says it in a way that's actually almost agitated with me, rather than the humored reaction I had expected.

"No no, that's not what I mean. I just mean that it's crazy how much has happened since the last time we came here. I mean, you went to the hospital and that's huge, but my mom also strangely opened up to me, we've been spending more time with each other, we've talked about college, you're getting a little better…Blue, this is all amazing and I'm so happy."

"You're right. A lot has changed. I guess I just wish my brother didn't have to die and I didn't have to attempt suicide," he pauses to give me a playful shove and a halfway chuckle, "in order for us to hang out a little more. You mean a lot to me, Lacey. I just wish I'd been able to say something sooner about needing you. You're all I've really got now."

I know he would find some way to continue to blame himself if I said something, but I want to be able to just tell him that I wish that I'd noticed it all sooner, that'd I'd known something was wrong. But maybe he'd be right to try to blame himself. He would say something like, *"Oh how would you know?"* and *"I intentionally kept it from you, it's not like I made it easy for you to notice"* and *"I wish you knew sooner too, but I couldn't find the motivation to let you in."* I bite my tongue instead.

"I wish that I'd spent more time with you sooner. You seem to be doing better now, but all that's really changed is you've had a therapy session at the hospital, and we've hung out a whole bunch. If I hadn't been so focused on school and had actually bothered to care about my best friend, maybe we could've avoided some of it."

"But we can't go back to that now, not really."

"Do you think that if I had stuck around you would've been able to tell me?"

"I don't know, maybe. It's possible, I guess."

"If I had stuck around, do you think you still would've tried?"

"Honestly, it's hard to tell. It's possible, but I was pretty fucked up after Donte died. I'm still a little fucked up, y'know? Just a couple weeks ago we were up here. That's pretty damn recent."

"Do you think--?"

"Lacey, seriously," he interrupts me before I can finish my thought, "you didn't do anything to me. You not being around was because of school, and that's really important. Even if I do wish that you could've been here. But I think most of it was about Donte being gone, about the silence in my head being so loud without him around. Before he was gone, I was used to not seeing you all the time because you were already more than three years into high school. The only thing that changed is I didn't have anyone to talk to."

"Blue, I didn't know that it was THAT bad. I should've known."

"Lacey, before I get mad could you just shut up and listen? You couldn't have known! I keep saying that! Don't blame yourself because it isn't about you! It's about me and it's about my brother! For the love of--!"

"Hey! Who's up there?" There's a voice coming up from the ground level, a teenage boy's it sounds like.

For a moment Brigham is still super pissed, but then he starts to look mortified. Our hideout was spotted, and our secret wouldn't be much of a secret for much longer.

I had to risk a peer over the wall. Blue refused to do it out of fear they'd instantly know he was black, and he told me that I'd have a better chance at not getting caught. I may be the dark kind of Chinese, but you saw more white kids that had my skin tone than his. I was about as middle ground as we could get at this point.

I looked down and saw a group of no more than seven down below. A couple of them I thought I could've recognized. It's possibly the gay couple that lives across the street from me, Marshal and Weedo? Of course, they aren't broadly known as that. People call him Weedo just because he's constantly high, and I've never walked past him without smelling Mary Jane. The only reason I even know about it is because I accidentally saw them making out by the dumpsters at school. When I caught them, they essentially pinned me down and made me swear not to tell anyone. The only reason no one knows is because Weedo holds hands with a girl at school. He calls her his *beard*, I think. Something about using her and pretending to be straighter or manlier or something. I guess it makes sense that she's called a beard?

I don't even know her name, but it kept everyone off his trail for a long fucking time. Marshal's parents got caught in a car crash pretty early on in his life, so now Marshal lives with Weedo and Weedo's parents while his dad serves time in jail for "accidentally" killing his wife. They must both be closeted to Nail because they're part of the gang, but I know that if anyone else found out they'd both be booted. Now that I'm one of the only people they're out to, one of them will come by the house once in a blue moon (or slightly more, let's be honest) whenever they're fighting over the fact that Weedo even has a girl he uses to pretend to be straight, or about all the weed, or anything else.

And another one might be the boy that lives two doors down from me. He happens to get beat up by his mom a lot, Julia. What's his name? Michael. Michael Thompson. I have such a hard time remembering his first name because he goes by Thompson instead. Apparently, his dad went by "Big Mikey" and Thompson has some sort of bone to pick with him. Thompson likes to wear big red hoodies and baggy pants and to keep his head down. The only reason I even know about his mom beating him is because he ran out of his house once with a black eye screaming that his mom was a monster. Everyone else was either at work or in their houses, but I was outside waiting to see Brigham. I don't think he remembers me. And I mean I don't think that he remembers me in general. My sitting on the sidelines while he ran away from his screaming mother was probably fleeting. At least Marshal and Weedo make semi-frequent visits.

At this point, I don't know if anyone recognizes me, but me sticking my neck out has clearly garnered their attention. Their eyes are squinting, and their necks are tilting their heads back to try and figure out who I might be.

"Hey, fucker! Are you gonna fucking answer me?"

I pull my head back behind the lip of the wall and look at Brigham with some panic. His eyes have widened, and his lower lip is slightly quivering. Logistically I know that the loss of the rooftop won't mean the end of anything special. We're here for closure and, hopefully, we weren't planning on coming back here very often. We have other private places we could go to. We could go to the beach or into my bedroom or right outside the town's border–if we could manage to sneak past the policemen–and beyond and we would be fine.

But I could tell that this would be emotionally scarring for Blue. I mean like, clearly this is the place of a lot of deliberation. Of course, what he deliberated didn't happen almost at all in the way that he wished it would, but who wouldn't be attached to that sort of thing? Most people who are depressed, I imagine, put a lot of work into their plans for death and get to be pretty nostalgic for it. That's how most people get to be about life-changing decisions, aren't they?

"Fucking answer me! We aren't gonna leave until you tell me how you got up there!"

I whisper to Blue, "We have to tell them how we got up here or they will NOT leave us alone!"

"You think I don't know that?" he breathes back to me. "I'm trying to think of a way to do that without getting fucking shot!"

The leader of this group shouts back up, "What, do you have a friend up there? Tell me what you know!"

"Why do they even want this place?" I practically mouth.

"It's supposed to be a prime spot to the gangs. They want to take it as a vantage point for when they fight. I guess you could also store a lot here. I don't know, why wouldn't they want to have access to a big abandoned hotel that they wouldn't have to pay rent on?"

"I guess that's true enough. But why do people even want to join these things? It takes so much time and it just hurts everyone, doesn't it? How would you even get into one?"

"I guess friends of friends? If you know someone and you feel like it then you're in, at least for Wood. Wouldn't surprise me if Nail intentionally recruited based off whoever serves them the most."

"Should we tell them how we got up here?"

"I mean we could, but this is kinda our place isn't it? I like it here. It's important to me. A lot of important shit happened here!"

"Blue, c'mon, don't you know that I already know that? But I'd rather not risk death over this rooftop. Let's just tell them."

"C'mon, they don't need this. If anything, Wood needs it more than they do. Regardless, I'd still rather keep this for just us."

"Blue, please! If we don't do this then we're stuck up here!" I yell whisper to him.

"Hey, fucker! Get down here or I'm calling the police on you for trespassing! Just tell us how to get up there!"

At this point, I have to give Blue one last look of desperation. "I know this place is important to you. I don't know why it ever wouldn't be with what's happened. But if either of us goes to jail for something like this, both of our plans for the future are fucked. There's no way the one time is gonna treat us well. We have to go down there."

And he finally nodded his head.

"Okay fine! We're coming down!"

"So the fucker, she speaks!"

We get down from the building a different way than we climbed up. I suppose that's convenient for a person who doesn't want to give away how to get into the building. We wind up taking the stairs down to the second story, and a window in the back is partially opened. We have to jump out onto surprisingly soft dirt onto the first floor. Don't get me wrong, it hurt like hell, but it could've been worse. I'm sure it hurts much less for Brigham because he typically gets out this way, but the last time I left the building I went down a firefighter's ladder from a second story window. I guess that's how they got up to the rooftop without being able to break down any doors or walls.

Nail doesn't see where we come out, so we have to circle around to the front of the building in order to show them that we've actually come down. The first thing that one of them says is "Oh it's a chink and a ni--"

He would've finished the statement, but Marshal punches him in the shoulder (pretty hard, actually) and he shuts up fast. I can tell that the guy that got hit wants to start a fight right then and there, but Weedo pulls him back and Thompson holds Marshal back and another guy that I don't recognize tells them both to "shut up! Do you guys want the hotel or not?"

I guess Marshal has a lot of pull with this particular sub-section of Nail, because he's the one that approaches us and asks us about how to get to the top of the hotel. "Lacey?" he starts when he finally gets a good look at me. "How the fuck did you get up there? You and Brigham Blue! How you doin' man?"

Marshal tries to give Brigham one of those dude hugs where people hit each other on the back but don't actually hug, but it turns out to be really awkward because Brigham doesn't really reciprocate the enthusiasm that Marshal does.

What Marshal even does with Nail is a huge question to me, just because he's always been one of the nicest white people I've ever known. Maybe Weedo pulled him in out of fear? It's difficult to tell. Maybe it's also just the two of them trying to look straight to the rest of the white folks in Pennyworth.

"If I had known it was the two of you, I would've made them quit calling you fuckers. I won't have them calling you anymore bullshit." He kinda looks back at the rest of the group at that point. And I don't know exactly the face that he makes at them, but he must have been pretty pissed at them. When he turns back to look at us again, his face is smiling. "I know that we want to know how to get up to the top of this hotel, but I would've never guessed that you two knew how to get up there!"

I respond with, "I didn't even know that the hotel was such a big deal. We just kinda hang out here and figured out how to get to the top pretty much by chance."

"We'll figure out how to get up there, eventually, right? But for now, how about we agree to meet up later? I've got it in good with the bouncer at the bar on the edge of town, the one by the pier."

"I mean, we could, but we don't even have fakes or anything to get in."

"Don't worry about that for now. It'll be a little difficult to convince Tony to let you guys in, but he owes me a favor anyway. If you guys wanna meet up after school tomorrow, we can get your pics taken and I'll have fake IDs within a week. Tony won't even remember your faces tonight."

At this point, Brigham and I both feel pretty skeptical about the situation, and I can tell that Marshal thinks that we don't trust Nail very much. After a while of trying to convince us, Brigham and I concede and agree to meet up at the bar at 10:30. One of the guys I don't recognize says to wear something short and tight. I try to pretend I didn't hear.

And on the bike ride home I can tell that Brigham is worried out of his mind for the two of us. Like, what the hell are we supposed to expect? I've only gotten drunk once before, and that was when I was too little to know what liquor was and had a helluva lot of it when my mom wasn't looking. Since then I've stayed away from it, afraid that something bad will happen again. I mean, my mom knew she couldn't take me to the hospital for alcohol poisoning or anything or else she wouldn't get to keep me for being a bad parent or something, even though she didn't do anything to get me drunk. She had to try and deal with it like I was a normal age drinker, and there was a lot (a LOT) of vomiting on my part. Luckily all of this went down over the summer, so I didn't miss any school, but I spent the better part of a week in bed trying to escape and avoid dehydration.

"Blue?"

"Yeah, Lace?"

"What have we gotten ourselves into?"

"That's a good question. I guess I'd rather go there and find out what they're up to. That sounds better than dealing with the potential consequences of not showing up. I mean, Marshal knows where you live."

"What's gonna change tonight?"

"Hopefully less than the two of us are thinking. Maybe nothing will happen at all. Maybe Marshal is genuinely being nice to you, Lace."

"I mean, I guess, but he has nothing to gain from my going to the bar."

"Whatever happens, I'm coming with you."

CHAPTER 6

FIRSTS

———

I decided pretty early on that all I would be wearing to the bar was going to be jeans and a t-shirt. It'd be nicer than shorts, but I wasn't planning on impressing anyone, especially not the idiot who told me to wear something tight. I'll never know if he was actually flirting or if he was just trying to look cool in front of his friends, but I'm not impressed. The only people I'd consider dating out of that handful of people is maybe Thompson or Marshal. Thompson because he kept a fight from happening with the douche nozzle that hit on me and actually looked like he cared about more than getting up to the roof. Marshal because I know that he actually cares about me. The only thing that would actually keep me from dating him is the fact that he's taken by Weedo.

Marshal isn't even totally gay, he's bi. And I used to have a major crush on him when I was younger, but it kinda died down.

Marshal used to visit the neighborhood all the time when we were all younger, just to visit Weedo (back when he still went by Will). They used to be the only ones that would play with me in the neighborhood. I only really know that he's bi because he brought it up once. Something about how fucking hot one of his old babysitters was. It didn't even really come up in conversation, and he just couldn't contain himself about it.

He and Weedo have been together for so long that it seems unlikely that they won't be together by the time I go to college and beyond. I hope I get invited to the wedding though. Will they ever get married? I mean, I can hope so, but gay marriage would never slide here, even if it's allowed in America. They'd just get harassed too much, I think. Maybe, just because it isn't terribly common, they won't even feel the need to. They'd have to move out of town in order to be open about it. And even if there were a courthouse in town, the two of them probably wouldn't be allowed to get married in the first place, even if the laws somehow do change. They'd be shut out by family, at the very least. Maybe hunted down by Nail. Hit harder by the police. Yeah, not unless they decided to pick up and leave town.

I feel kinda bad, knowing that it might be a long time before Marshal and Weedo get the chance to be recognized by the law. I mean, obviously, the best part of loving someone isn't the tax breaks or whatever pros come with marriage. It's the love part and the togetherness part and the working to make shit work part, but still. I guess it's the principle. And that's what I'm thinking of when I walk up to the bar and tap Marshal on the shoulder. Part of me was hoping no one would show and that it would all be a joke. But that was clearly too much to hope, especially if Nail wanted the hotel. It would've been nice to show up and have been in the clear though, like if Marshal had told the other guys to back off and let us go. Well, a deal's a deal.

He turns around and greets me with a smile once I finally get his attention. And then he nods at the bouncer, who I'm guessing is Tony, and I get let into the bar. At first, I'm overwhelmed, and then I'm completely and utterly underwhelmed. The first thing I noticed was the smell. Everyone in the place smelled like they were sweating beer and tequila. And then I scanned the room for anyone that I recognized. I tried to find Thompson or Weedo or Blue, but I couldn't tell who anyone in any of the booths were. I didn't think it would be that hard to find a group of seven white guys with a black guy in the middle of a bar, but it looked kinda like Brigham hadn't even bothered to show up.

I try to look for anyone I might recognize. Where's Weedo's lemon juice dyed hair? Where's Thompson's red sweatshirt? The guy that flirted with me, he had a neck tattoo, where's that thing? I thought about going back outside to ask Marshal where everyone was, but then I got stopped in my tracks.

Weedo came up behind me and offered me a drink.

"Here, drink up".

I practically jumped two feet into the air out of surprise. I had no idea what was in it, but I reflexively took the glass out of his hand anyway.

Trying not to drop the glass, I ask, "Weedo, where's Brigham?"

"He's back at the booth with the others, but we haven't discussed anything yet. Tomorrow we're still planning on getting you those fakes, right?"

"I guess. I mean I think so. Wait should I go to the table?"

"No no, don't worry about it for right now. Brigham'll come and get you when we need you. For now, the boys are gonna talk."

"What the fuck does that mean?"

"Oh, come on. It's not like that. Brigham told me that he was the one who figured out how to get to the rooftop and that he'd tell us all about it. You don't gotta be there to talk about that, you'd get bored. You already know how to get up there."

"I mean, I guess?"

"Go have a good time, alright?"

"Wait, I still don't know what's happening here. What's with getting us to the bar and whatever the fuck? You could've just asked us straight up how to get to the roof this afternoon."

"Chill, okay? Marshal wanted to do something nice for you kids. We like you, alright? Go have fun. That chick's been making eyes at you since you got in here."

At that point, he's shoved me (playfully?) vaguely in the direction of the bar. There's a girl there with red hair and a smattering of freckles across her cheeks. She's definitely looking at me, but it's difficult to tell if she's actually been looking at me for that long. I don't know if I've held her attention for very long. She's probably only looking at me because Weedo pushed me into her general direction.

By the time that I keep myself from falling and start walking vaguely normally again, she's laughing at me. There's an empty stool right next to her, and I halfway stumble into it. It's not even the fact that I'm particularly nervous to speak with a new person, but the awkwardness of being pushed in this direction and sitting down next to a stranger looks a particular way.

Y'know those scenarios in television shows and movies where a character's friend will have to physically push them to talk to someone they're interested in dating? It looks like that.

"Hi, sorry my friend basically shoved me out of a conversation with 'the boys' and apparently I'm not needed."

"Heh, that's alright. I get it."

"I'm Lacey, by the way."

"I'm Rosalyn. I think my mom might've brought up a Lacey recently? Were you at the hospital over the last couple of weeks? Meet a Gracie? A Sadie?"

"Yeah, the Cliffords, I think?"

"I'm Sadie's little sister and Gracie's daughter. I guess we were supposed to somehow run into each other at the diner or at school, but I have no idea how we were supposed to recognize each other. There are so many Asian chicks at school."

"I mean, Sadie told me to keep a lookout for a pretty girl with freckles and red hair, but I must've been paying really poor attention. I haven't seen many redheads at school."

"Hah. She thinks I'm pretty?"

"Yeah, and I think I agree with her. I mean, have you seen yourself?"

"Thanks, heh." She clearly gets a little bit flustered and turns her head slightly away from me. There's a little bit of awkward silence until I break it.

"So Weedo told me that he saw you staring at me. What's up with that?" I try to be good-natured about it, let her know that I'm just teasing her and seeing what buttons I can poke.

"Oh, your friend saw that? I mean, he isn't wrong. I haven't seen you here before, and I guess I thought I knew all the kids with fakes at school."

"I don't even have a fake, apparently Tony owed Marshal a favor? I certainly didn't buy this drink for myself."

"Hey, hey, hey. You got yourself a freebie. Sure Weedo doesn't have the hots for little ole you?"

"Hah, no no he's entirely gay. In case you couldn't tell."

"Hah, 'course I could. What kind of lesbian would I be if I didn't have a halfway decent gaydar?"

I'm a little caught off guard. Should I have a... gaydar? I try to play along, "Hmm, that's fair. I guess that's why Sadie didn't say anything about your boyfriend when I met her a couple weeks ago. Although, she didn't say anything about a girlfriend, either."

"Oh yeah? That seems like her."

"What do you mean? Is she homophobic or some shit like that?"

"No, she's just the kind to spare me of my embarrassment," she chuckles a little bit, "I haven't dated anyone since last year, it's been awhile. Nice of her to not say anything."

"Well, I wish that she had. Then I could've known you were single sooner."

"What's it to you?"

"You're pretty. And you seem really sweet. And your family already likes me. I'd like to get to know you better, y'know?" How forward of me.

The two of us spent a lot of time speaking last night, but nothing else really happened. We talked about seeing each other again. We got really excited. And just in case anyone was wondering, it looks like the conversation that the guys had with Brigham never really ended. They didn't need me. And I know that he's safe because Marshal was there, so he probably wound up safe.

The last bit of the night is a blur to me, and I feel what must be a hangover setting in. And I don't know where I am. I look around and everything is just… nice. There are pressed linens and clean white sheets on the bed. The curtains on the window look like they're more than just practical. The room is bigger than my bedroom. Where am I? Where's Rosalyn?

I know this isn't Brigham's house, and it certainly isn't mine. It wouldn't be Weedo's place, 'cuz there's no way that it's this nice in comparison to where my mom and I live.

Before I even think about getting out of bed, there's a knock at the door and I see Rosalyn sneaking in. What day is today? Have I missed school?

Rosalyn holds her finger to her lips and comes over to the bed. The rest of the house must be asleep. Or empty. And she suddenly climbs in under the covers with me, pressing her lips into mine.

Maybe there's part of last night that I don't completely remember.

I pull myself away after a moment, mostly attempting to connect the dots as to what had happened in the last twelve hours. I only remember talking for several hours, but there are a lot of gaps. I don't remember leaving or coming here or falling asleep. I only really remember a lot of talking and then seeing Brigham briefly when he asked if needed a ride home, and then Rosalyn introduced herself. I don't think I ever answered him. I think he just left. I don't know if Rosalyn said she'd take me home. I don't remember having more than the drink that Weedo handed me. I don't remember a lot of things.

"Rosalyn, what happened last night?" Is what I tried to say. But she dove back in and tried to kiss me again.

"Come on, let's start from where we left off, huh?" She said this part slyly.

"Wait."

She didn't listen to me. How horny was she? She starts to pin me down in the bed.

"Wait."

I start squirming under the weight of her. Have I always been this small? She's pushing her mouth onto mine. It feels slimy.

"Hey, hold on."

My heart is beating really hard. Does she think I'm kidding? One hand is hard on my left shoulder, the other is fiddling with the jeans I've been wearing since last night.

"Rosalyn."

She's gotten them halfway down my thighs now.

"Hey, hey, what're you doing?"

I'm trying not to scream, and my vision is blurring. My breathing feels really shallow.

"Can you stop?" Slimy lips. "Rosalyn." Can't breathe. "I really don't like this." One hand over my mouth as she pulls my panties down and gets both them and my jeans around my knees. I feel something plunge into me, but, oh god, it hurts really bad. What's stabbing me? I can't see anything, not clearly.

She finally speaks, "Why do you always talk so much whenever we do this? It's not like I even got anything from you last night. You act like you don't even enjoy it."

She's flabbergasted at me, as if she's surprised that I'm not okay. What is inside of me? Why is she pushing down on my mouth so hard? I'm completely frozen and I'm terrified. Why can't I move? What's going on?

"I mean, what gives, Lacey? Aren't you into me? You were the one that started kissing me last night."

Did I really do that? How drunk did I get?

Suddenly she plunges her fingers into me really deeply, and the pain is crazy. How many are in there? *Ow. Fuck. Ow. Fuck. OwFuck. OwFuck. OwFuck. Owfuckfuckfuckfuckfuck.*

She doesn't even have her hands on my arms or anything. I could push her off and get away. Why can't I move? Fuck. I don't know how long it goes on for. I guess Rosalyn really knows what she wants out of me. I can't tell if I'm bleeding or not, but my thighs feel wet.

She stops suddenly.

"You came even faster than last night. Wow, I must be getting good at this!"

She looks proud of herself.

I think I'm crying.

I've spent the last few minutes staring at the old light on the ceiling. It's one of those round ones where the fixture looks like a bowl, and there's a gap between the lip of the glass and the ceiling. One of the ones where, if a fly winds up dying in there, you can see it through on the other side when the light is on. There's one in there now. Or maybe it's just dirty.

"Woah, wait are you crying? Was it that good?"

I keep lying there. I feel so vulnerable. Before I realize how I reach the position, I'm on my left side and hugging my knees to my chest. I feel my chest shaking and blood rushing into my cheeks from all the deep breaths I've been taking. My pussy feels really sore.

She shoves three fingers in my face, and they're all moist. They're all a little shiny. For some reason, they're tinged pink. I don't think she realizes that I'm bleeding yet. "Look it, these were all inside of you! Isn't that cool?"

How is she so oblivious?

Gracie and Sadie must've both been at work early in the morning, cuz I never hear a footstep in the house. By the time that I can speak, she suddenly seems like she cares, and that's only after she realizes that I'm too upset to get her off too. Is that what sex is like? If it is, I don't want it.

"Rosalyn, did we do that last night too?"

"I mean, of course we did. What else do YOU do when you're drunk?"

"I've never been drunk before."

"What, really? I guess that explains it. You're such a light-weight, I'm surprised you started with a long island."

"So that's what that was." And then there's a long pause before I can collect my thoughts enough to say anything. "That made me really uncomfortable. It hurt a lot. I'd never kissed anyone before you, or done anything like that, even with myself."

"Wait, what? So now you regret it? I got you off twice and had to rub myself out last night!"

"Dude, this wasn't cool. I'm in a lot of pain right now. I don't know if you noticed or not, but there's literally a puddle of blood on these sheets." I move over so that she can see the damage more clearly, and I smear it a little on the way off. It's a lot of blood.

"Wait, wait, wait. No, no, no." She gasps as if she's finally gotten it. "I'm such a cunt. I did that to you. Fuck. Wait, so when you were telling me to wait earlier, you were serious?"

"Yeah, seems like it. You had to pin me down and cover my mouth to get me to shut up, remember?"

"But you didn't struggle the entire time. I thought it was role play or something. Oh god oh god oh god."

"Did it ever cross your mind that I didn't want to do anything? Like at all? Why else would I say all that to you earlier?" Earlier I was terrified. I don't know what I am now. I'm caught somewhere in between crying and wanting to scream.

"Woah, don't get so mad at me. I didn't know. I'd done that kind of thing a couple times before and I didn't think it would be a big deal. You seem like the kind of person who'd wanna be dominated."

"Hey fuck you. I didn't need you to be my fucking dominatrix. I've never even had sex before, you idiot!" Everything feels like it's spinning. How much blood did I lose? How much am I losing? The spot looks like more than I would get on a heavier period day. Fuck.

"Don't call me a fucking idiot! You were throwing yourself on me last night! You kissed me, remember? I didn't know! Holy fuck!"

"You know what, I don't care right now. I just wanna go home. Can I borrow your phone? I need to call my friend."

"No no no." She says this like she's a pissed off mom talking down to her teenager. "We're not done talking about this. Apologize to me! You never said anything and you're making me feel like shit for it!"

"I'm not fucking apologizing for anything! If you really think this is my fault, fine." At this point, I get up out of the bed and I storm out of the room, still ass naked. I'm looking for pads and a pair of jeans that I can borrow, since mine are stained with blood.

"What the fuck are you doing? We're talking!"

"Where are your pads? And get me a pair of your jeans."

"Are you serious?" She stares at me in disbelief. It's like she can't believe someone wouldn't want to worship at her feet for the chance to fuck her. She stomps off to a place that must be her bedroom and slams the door.

I hurry to the bathroom and look under the sink to find the pads, and I run into another bedroom to borrow some jeans. This must be Sadie's room. It's as nice as the room I must've spent the night in. There are just some more personal touches. There's a desk in here, and a decorated cork board with lots of pictures of her and Rosalyn when the two of them were younger. There are some that have Gracie in them. And some with a man that must not be around anymore. At a closer glance, I realize he's someone I recognize.

CHAPTER 7

MISTER

——

I'll spare you the gory details of sneaking into the guest room and grabbing my bloodied panties and jeans. But I will say that something odd compelled me to take pictures of the blood on the bed. There was a package with a brand new throw away camera in Sadie's room, and I used that to take pictures of what I could. I'm almost glad that they had carpet flooring instead of wood or laminate. It kinda makes me feel like Gracie and Sadie will see it when they get home unless Rosalyn acts fast.

When Brigham pulls up to the house, I run like my life depends on it. I nearly collapse into him before he can try and talk me into riding his handlebars. He plays it safe and we walk for a while. I tell him what happened.

I don't see much of the neighborhood on the way out. It's mostly a blur of tall houses with big, well-kept yards and fresh coats of white or tan paint. No drywall patches, I don't think. Not any that I could see. I notice that the street rides more smoothly too. Everything seems so bright—almost like it should be cheerier.

"Lace, you should go to the police station. Make a report. Do something about it."

"Blue, I don't know if I can." I'm in so much physical pain. I also just can't wrap my head around what just happened. What just happened?

"Come on. I don't think that anyone has ever made a report before and been successful. They always wait too long. Or the police have some other shitty excuse for why they can't go through with things. This is your chance!" He seems so passionate about it. I know that it's because he's worried.

"I don't know. I don't think I can."

I've had my first kiss and I don't even remember it, just hours later. This is something I was supposed to be excited about.

He eases up on me, "Okay." He breathes really heavily through gritted teeth. "I'm sorry. I know it has to be a lot."

"A lot." I guess it was a lot. Am I a virgin anymore?

He tells me that he'll take me home and make the police report after I get there. And so I hand him the throwaway camera with the pictures of the bloody bed on them and he tells me that he'll have to get them developed first. I don't know how it'll work. What if Blue is suspected of doing everything to me? I wouldn't put it beyond the policemen to do that.

I try to tell him over and over not to do anything, but I can't. He doesn't listen. It doesn't work. Maybe this time he'd be lucky. Maybe this time we'd be listened to.

Part of me feels obligated to go, but part of me feels like I shouldn't move any more than I have to. I feel tears rolling down my cheeks. Everything feels like a dream. This isn't real, right?

As soon as I get home, I realize how quiet it is.

I unlock the door and zombie walk into my bedroom and lay down.

What time is it? Already after noon. I haven't eaten anything all day. I'm exhausted.

I climb into my bed and don't even bother to wash off, even though I feel like my entire body is dirty. Everything feels like it sticks to itself and its surroundings. I can't pull my fingers apart from each other and they're almost glued to my stomach. I want to throw up. I don't. I fall asleep.

Luckily when I fell asleep, I was on my side. I woke up four hours later to Brigham in my bedroom cleaning vomit off my floor. There's a stream of it coming down on my sheets, but it's not a lot. Regardless of how much there is on the sheets, they'll have to be washed, preferably without my mom finding out. If Valerie Wong found out her daughter had been drinking, she would kill her. And in this case, "her" would be me. But I wish I could say something to her, just because she's my mom and everything. Maybe I can find a way to talk to Gracie without running into Rosalyn. Maybe I can talk to Sadie.

Maybe it's for the best that Rosalyn and I won't work out. I mean, besides the obviousness of the whole...thing from last night. But logistically too. I knew that dad had a new girlfriend after he and my mom had broken up, but I didn't know that he had been dating Gracie. I didn't know that until after I saw the pictures in Sadie's room anyway.

I don't think I'm ready to get situated with a family that also knew my dad. In a way, it'd be like talking to stepsisters and having a stepmom. And Rosalyn spent the rest of the time this morning storming off into her room refusing to help me and yelling at me over and over again that I couldn't possibly blame her for something she didn't think to consider. I couldn't possibly talk about being violated by her since she was putting my pleasure before her own.

Is that how it really went down, though?

Maybe I wasn't clear enough. Or maybe she's right and I really do regret doing stuff with her and that's why I'd maybe say that she raped me. And she just accidentally cut me up on the inside without knowing she was hurting me. And maybe I just think I remember the pain.

Is all of that possible? I mean I never straight up said no.

But I'm so sure right now that I never wanted any of that.

I pushed her off me this morning, right? When she tried to kiss me?

I kept trying to get her to listen to me, didn't I?

And didn't I feel frozen?

I couldn't move. This all happened like less than five hours ago. Maybe four.

When did I wake up?

It's a really long time before I can say anything to Brigham. I moan a little when I first wake up. He must know that I'm awake when I do that, before I even knew that he's in the room and the smell of vomit hits me square in the nose. What could I have possibly thrown up? I haven't eaten anything this morning. But it's still there and it's more than just bile.

When I open my eyes, I look at Brigham like he's my saving grace or something. He's busy at work, taking care of me.

"So what did they say at the police station?"

"I had to get the pictures developed before I could do anything else. That took about an hour. And when I got to the station, for a long while they wouldn't take me. But then the chief of police came out and heard them yelling at me and me arguing with them. He told me his name was Jacob Smith and brought me into his office. I showed him the pictures and I told him everything that you told me."

"Did he believe you?"

"He told me to come back as soon as I can with you. He thinks that you'll be able to better explain."

"Oh…" When he tells me that I'll have to talk about what happened again, it's like my body almost freezes up. I'm terrified of having to talk about it. Most of me doesn't want to believe that everything really happened. A part of me doesn't even know if I made up how I was feeling in the midst of it or not. *I mean, I orgasmed right? I must've secretly wanted it, right?*

"I don't know if I can."

"Lacey, I know that it's hard. But this needs to happen. I think that this Jacob Smith guy might actually make it so that she gets punished. Who knows who else she's done this shit to? Lace, look at me."

He grabs my chin and makes me look him in the eyes.

"I know that you didn't want any of this to happen. You were assaulted. I have never seen you more terrified in your life than how you looked this morning when I came to get you. What Rosalyn did is not okay."

I was scared. I was terrified. He said so. I didn't want it. I didn't want it. Why can't I believe it when Brigham says it? He wouldn't lie to me. He knows better. He knows me.

"I-- I'll do it then, Blue. Let's go."

He has to help me sit up, I'm so shaky. But I manage to stand without too much of his help. And I take a step forward. For a second I consider the vomit-stained sheets and pull them off the bed. They aren't due to be washed until later this week, but I can spot clean them and let them hang dry. Tell my mom I got a bloody nose while I was taking a nap. *Don't let her worry.*

The cleaning and scrubbing gives me something to focus on without thinking too much about what has happened. I mean, clearly the vomit came from something, but there were moments where I could just clean and treat it all like everything was normal. Maybe I can believe the bloody nose story for a moment. Maybe I can pretend like nothing happened once I'm done talking to this Jacob Smith guy.

Since the throw up is fresh it comes out in less than ten minutes without a lot of hard scrubbing. Brigham actually takes slightly longer than that to finish cleaning up after me on the laminate near my bedside. We'll have to chuck the ruined rags in a neighbor's trash can before we go, but we leave quickly. Once the bedsheets are hanging up to dry, we head to the front of the house and out the door.

Riding on the handlebars of Brigham's bicycle doesn't elicit any mighty yawps out of either of us today. I'm mostly just exhausted and really scared about what lies ahead.

"It's really strange for a victim of rape to not come along to report the incident, though I suppose I can understand why you'd rather go home and try to sleep it off. I think that I would do that, if I were in your position."

"Yeah, I guess there wasn't much else I could imagine doing. Some of me wonders whether I actually remember it correctly and if I made it up in my head or not."

"What do you mean?"

"I mean like, obviously everything happened or else I wouldn't have wound up at her house and I wouldn't have bled everywhere and felt so terrified I needed to call Brigham to pick me up and take me home."

"Right, Mr. Mathis has filled me in on that." Officer Smith sounds so calm. Not robotic, like I'd expected. He's almost kind?

"But I'm starting to wonder if I actually didn't want to be a part of it. I mean, this girl said that I came, so I must've wanted it. Right?"

"I don't know what elicited that. There's a lot I don't know about the female body–that just isn't anything I've learned about–but it does sound like you experienced a lot of pain and discomfort. That's clear because of the amount of blood that's present in the pictures and in the clothes Mr. Mathis brought to me. This case is in better shape than most that I get."

"Yeah, right. I didn't want it. I remember feeling frozen."

"I know that most of the guys in this office wouldn't believe you and would just tell you that because you 'came,' as you put it. But I think that this is something that should be taken seriously. A lot of rape stories don't make it very far in the court process, just in general. And, when it comes from Pennyworth, it's even less. You have pictures, you have other physical evidence. I'll do what I can to get this all underway. Unless you decide that you don't want to go through with filing the petition and heading to court, that is."

I'm quiet for a moment. I could be strong and actually make a difference, try to set a precedent in Pennyworth somehow. But then I could also just give in. I'd really rather not talk about it. And how long would all of this really take?

"This'll be a lengthy process, Miss Matthews. I wouldn't blame you for not going through with it. But if you think that people would be safer without the assailant living in freedom, and if you're up for the challenge, I think there would be a lot of change started up here."

I have to pause and think for a long while. First of all, why in the world is this cop being so kind to me? And what about college? What about my future and getting out of this town? "I want to go to college in the fall. It would be at the community college a couple of towns out, and I would have to live there. How would this change that?"

"I can get guys out to the house of the assailant within the next few weeks, she'll be held here–it's a she right? That's just crazy to me, god–and then within the next three days she'd have to testify to me and whoever else I put on the case. Then within a couple of weeks, we'd have a preliminary hearing where a lawyer might have you testify. We'd provide you with a prosecutor, of course, if you couldn't afford one."

"Oh, god, I'd have to tell my mom what happened. She's so busy with work and everything already. I can't—"

"That might not be a problem. She wouldn't have anything much to do at the preliminary hearing, if we had one. It'd be cutting it close, but we might be done with your case before the summer ends. There should be no problem with you going to college in the fall. I'm going to make sure that I'm as up close and personal on this case as I possibly can be, alright, Miss Matthews?"

"Thank you, Mister…" I blank on his name for a moment. And by the time that I finally remember he responds.

"It's Mr. Smith, but Mister is alright too. I'll send some guys out about now, is that alright, Miss Matthews?"

It might all be over before school starts. And I might be able to start school late if I really really have to. Oh god, what has happened to Brigham and me so recently? Fuck. "That'd be alright, Mister." I nod my head in thanks and approval as he ushers Brigham and me out of his office.

"After I get a few things organized for an arrest warrant for Miss Clifford--Rosalyn, right?--I'll take you to the forensic lab. We'll get some swabs of what we can off you to collect evidence for the case. Then we can send you home and you can get cleaned up. You're in good hands with me, don't worry."

This is officially the nicest interaction I've ever had with a cop, like ever. Brigham and I stand next to Mister, holding hands with each other like he's giving me some kind of strength to keep going, while Mister gives orders to a couple of policemen who are on call. I recognize a handful of them, and I even begin to wonder which one of them might've shot my dad nine years ago. He sends two of them to their offices to wait for further instructions to organize an arrest warrant for Rosalyn Clifford.

CHAPTER 8

BETTER

———

The only thing that I could do for a couple of days was lie in bed and figure out what was going on. But I didn't tell my mom, just because I felt like I couldn't. Would she judge me? I've always been yelled at to not drink, and now I'm so terrified... What if she just judges me for drinking and that outweighs the fact that I bled out half a cup of blood because another person decided to shove their fingers into my pussy? And it shouldn't outweigh that, but in my irrational mind, it does.

I pretended to be sick, horrendously sick until Wednesday morning, where my mom told me that I had gotten "miraculously better" enough to go back to school. I guess my pretending wasn't that difficult. It was still hard to hold on to food, so I threw up a lot. And I spent so much time under the covers that my body was really, really warm whenever my mom came into my bedroom. I hadn't even seen Brigham since the day that we went to the police together.

The first thing I did Wednesday morning, once I had returned to campus, was scope out the school for Rosalyn. I saw two redheads the entire day, and neither of them was Rosalyn. At lunch I overheard a group of girls speaking in hushed voices, and all they could talk about was how Rosalyn wasn't there that day, and did they miss a really big assignment, and how sick must she be to not be here all day, and why isn't she returning texts or calls?

And all I can think about is the fact that it can only mean one thing: the police got the arrest warrant and got her out of the house sometime between school ending yesterday and school starting this morning. Oh yeah, and I suspect no one really cared about the fact that I was gone. The girls I eat lunch with are... well, they're all like me.

They're all Asian. They're all petite. They're all very smart. And when they're at school all they ever talk about is school. I've only ever seen them outside of school to work on school projects because I had to, and I'm pretty sure they all spend other time with each other outside of school. I've heard them refer to me as their friend before, but I wouldn't call them that. I could never say that they aren't friends of mine to anyone—just in case word got around—but they'll never know that. They're people I know. And all they discuss is school. And they don't ask what kept me at home all weekend and halfway through the week.

I finish lunch quickly and go to the school office where they let kids borrow the school phone line, and I lie to get access to it since it's typically only used for emergencies. I call Brigham's cell phone number and tell him to come and get me after school. When I hang up, the office ladies tell me that they hope I feel better, and I thank them while considering the burgeoning acting career I'd have. But then, in times of dire need like mine, who wouldn't lie their ass off to keep people from asking. I was barely okay with speaking to Mister about the situation, and the only other person who knows me well enough to know everything else about me is Brigham. Why the fuck would I tell other people about this shit? I have one person and the police, and that's all a girl really needs, right?

When school ends, I find Brigham at the front of the school waiting for me, bike and all and just like he has the last few weeks. I don't know how I used to do this thing where I walked home by myself every fucking day without saying more than a couple of sentences to acquaintances at school and just doing homework in a darkish room at home and only coming out for meals. I was fucking lonely until Brigham attempted suicide.

And now that I've been assaulted, I know that I need him now more than ever. But what if I'd gotten assaulted somehow and we weren't in the swing of things? Well, actually, a lot of things would be different if we'd been in the "swing of things" all along. Maybe he wouldn't have attempted suicide. Then we wouldn't have the rooftop. We wouldn't have gone to that bar. I wouldn't have been fucking raped. And now my heart is beating out of my chest like *RE-gret RE-gret RE-gret RE-gret RE-gret RE-gret.* And as soon as I begin to notice that, it switches on me to *re-GRET re-GRET re-GRET.*

"Hey, Lace!"

Blue seems excited to see me after a few days, but then he gives me a once over and regrets it, like he remembers.

"Have you been okay? I've missed you a lot the last few days."

"Yeah, yeah I'm fine. It was just a rocky first day back, y'know?"

"What do you want to do today? I told Weedo and Marshal that we'd get our fakes sometime this week, but we could do it Saturday, if you wanted that instead."

"Or we can do it now." I wonder if I sound too apathetic.

"Oh, you wanna do it now? I didn't think you'd be so raring to go already."

"I mean there's nothing else that we have to do, right? And I don't have anything to worry about at the bar anymore right? She's been arrested."

Brigham looks like he's concerned about me. What's he worried about? I'm just tired of thinking about this assault thing and I don't fucking feel like wallowing anymore. "Okay, Lace. Let's get you into the neighborhood. But promise me we'll do something chill after."

Once we're both on the bike we head in the direction of my house.

"So what did you wanna do once we finish up across the street? You get to pick today." He sounds like he's speaking to me cautiously, like those teachers that talk down to you when they think you're stupid.

But I can't help but answer like I know he actually cares. "I don't know, really. We could go to the beach? I like it there."

And then he chuckles to himself, "At least you don't want to go to the rooftop. I'm sorta done with that place."

"So does Nail know how to get to the rooftop now?"

"Kinda. They tried to get me drunk so I'd talk, but I kinda just pretended to be drunk and gave them vague-ass answers. I think I told them to get the rope on the hook. They tried to press me for more, but I kept telling them that that's literally it. And, I mean, if you think about it, that's literally all you have to do to get into the building."

"Do you think that we should tell anyone in Wood about it? So they're on even ground with Nail? I know that they both want it."

"I'm afraid that people in Nail would just get pissed and there'd be a shoot-out or something between them. And who in Nail is just gonna tell the Woods how to get up there? Who would they suspect if they didn't suspect us?"

"Fuck. I mean if we were in a gang we'd obviously be in with the Woods, right? Feels like betrayal or something, even if we aren't in with them."

"But don't you know way more people in Nail? I mean you know Thompson, Marshal, Weedo. Your dad used to be in Nail, didn't he?"

"That's not the point. How many non-white people do you know of, just KNOW OF, in Nail?"

"I don't know. Maybe three or four that come by the diner? There might be a couple more that I've missed, but that's about all I've seen."

"Kinda makes you think that not all of the people *in* Nail are quite as nice as the people that we *care about* in Nail. Do you think Marshal and Weedo are out to ANYONE in Nail? Most of the people in Nail wind up in the police force, and we both know that they're racist as fuck. Mister might be the nicest person I've ever met in the police, by a really wide margin."

"Yeah, but we don't know anyone in Wood. Why does it matter to us? We could probably get into Nail if we wanted to."

"But we'd only get in because we're two colored kids who gave them an advantage over the other colored kids and they'd be trying to reward us for it. It'd be like the only way we're worth anything to them is if we lift them up while keeping the rest of 'our kind' from being lifted up too."

And he has to be quiet for a minute.

"It isn't just about us, Blue. It's about the rest of the people in this town that the police think they can take advantage of without getting hurt themselves. I know that we want to be okay, and we'll eventually have college. But what about the people that are super likely to wind up staying here just because they choose to? Or because they can't help but stay here because they have to?"

We get to Weedo's and Marshal's before he can answer me.

Brigham runs up to the door and raps on it, throwing his bike into my hands just as I manage to jump off. And he pumps his right leg incessantly until Weedo opens the door and tells us to call him William until we all got into the garage in the backyard, that his mom was home and she shouldn't hear.

Maybe it's not that he couldn't answer me, but more that he refused to. He seemed anxious to prove to me that people in Nail were alright, but I already know that that's the case. But he's desperate. He thinks he's found a way out of Pennyworth; he thinks he's found a way out of racism because the white guys like him. But I don't think he gets it yet. Maybe one way of fighting racism is working with the white guys, but you certainly don't combat it by pushing down the people that haven't been as fortunate. Brigham told me himself that Nail was racist as fuck, and once it sounded like he wouldn't be caught dead in that gang. We have some power over the white guys. Why can't we use it to the advantage of people like us? But this is a conversation for another time. It has to be. He's already disappeared into the house.

Weedo winks at me coyly as I move closer to the door, and I have to think about why for a moment before I remember. He's wondering about the girl with the fiery hair that he shoved me at several nights ago. He thinks that he's done me a solid.

Or maybe that's just Weedo.

"Thanks, William."

I walk through a kitchen with tiling and wooden countertops and one of the biggest fridges I've ever seen in my life and a dustpan leaning against the kitchen table. The kitchen is dusty despite the dustpan, but I don't pay much more mind to what's happening in the kitchen besides this. I'm quickly ushered into the backyard, which is surprisingly lush considering the way that the front yard looks. There's a large-ish tree supporting the weight of a tire swing, and there are a couple of flower beds that are decorated with roses and tulips and some other ones that are purple and that look curled up like a hundred little dancers.

And we sit out here for a little while, the four of us. They're kind enough to let me sit on the tire swing and don't pay any mind to the swinging that I do back and forth, back and forth. They all sit on the ground, and we make a square and just talk about anything. I've never been to Weedo's house before, and I've never seen him and Marshal be so calm around each other. They clutch each other's hands so easily now that Weedo's mom is out of their line of vision. I have to work hard to remember that they've been together for years, even if it's mainly been in secret.

They're so happy and comfortable with each other, that it hurts even more to talk about Rosalyn when Weedo says, "So how did you and that cute redhead hit it off the other day?"

He just seems so excited and certain, until I falter, and I don't say anything.

Blue tries to play it cool with, "Oh she'd rather not talk about it. Don't be--"

"Embarrassed? Coy? What? It wasn't good, and I don't really wanna talk about it." I feel my vision go blurry and something wet and warm hits my right check. Then my left. Right again.

"Holy fuck. What could've possibly happened to you?" Marshal essentially jumps up from his seat and runs to the opposite side of the square to hug me.

It takes a lot to not shove him off me, and a lot of settling in.

You're safe here.

You're okay.

He wouldn't hurt you.

Breathe in.

Breathe out.

"Brigham and I went to the police station the next morning. I woke up in her house, and the chief of police is calling it rape but I don't know if it really is or not. I don't even really think I know what happened." My body shudders as I finally take a deep breath in and out.

"Fuck."

Weedo has to run inside in order to calm down, and Marshal has to take Brigham and me into the garage for a change of pace. And somehow the storage shed that they call a garage, with the overstuffed couches and a too big table and a full sized and unmade bed–a place that should've made me feel totally claustrophobic and uncomfortable, a place of dirty and chaos and teenage boy–made me feel better.

I needed a darker place than what was outside. I needed to shut in and collapse and cry my eyes out and find a small space to squeeze into because, oddly, being in an open space made me feel too small. To be in a place as wide and open as a little backyard makes me feel like an ant, about to be crushed. It was like too many different points in the universe were pulling at my limbs, telling me to *fill up this space, be big enough for this space, you're not big enough or strong enough.* Small feels good. Well, it doesn't feel good. But there's less pulling. It feels better, anyway.

Before long Marshal is able to help me calm down. And I don't know if Weedo did calm down or not because he wasn't there. He wasn't there when I got my picture taken for my fake ID. And he wasn't there when Brigham got his picture taken for his fake ID. And he wasn't there when Marshal told me that it didn't really matter how bad crying made me look because no one is meant to look good in a state ID in the first place. And he wasn't there when Marshal pulled out what was just a foreign science experiment type thing and got to work on some sort of development thing that went toward making these little pieces of plastic that would give me access to more of those Long Island iced teas and those cushy bar stools and might let me see Rosalyn again--

I want to see her again.

We don't walk out with IDs, and we won't for another few days while Marshal and Weedo take care of development. I don't know how they learned to do this, but it's probably for the best that they don't use the singular computer in the library to look up that kind of stuff or get it done out of town. The line for that dinosaur is long, and it probably wouldn't be the best for that kind of information on a public computer. But whatever they did, however they did it, I've ceased to care. I'm just glad that they did.

Once I walk out of the garage, which I learn Marshal actually lives in instead of rooming with Weedo, outside doesn't feel like it's pulling as much. The opposite actually. I feel normal sized again, at least mostly.

But we still don't leave, not for a while. The time that I'd normally spend with just Brigham gives space for Marshal and an odd Wednesday evening. We talk about nothing in particular, and we laugh like we've known each other for years. Weedo doesn't leave the house, at least not until after I have to return home. And even if he came out immediately after I left, I don't see him until the next day at school. But then he doesn't grip the hand of his beard (I guess I really never learned her name) like he normally does, and he doesn't walk from class to class with Marshal either.

He just ducks his head down. He's ashamed, and I think this is the first time—other than when I saw him and Marshal making out with each other—that I've seen any sense of shame on his face. He didn't know who Rosalyn was. He just saw her as the girl at the bar with the red hair who had eyes for me once I stepped in. He didn't mean to hurt me, and I know that, but today he never lets me get close enough to say so. Whenever we run into each other and there are long breaks of silence, he asks if I need water and doesn't let me speak up. It's almost like he secretly knows that I can't blame him for what happened, but he continues to blame himself for what was truly unforeseen by any of us. He cuts me off before I can even breathe in to get ready.

For a little while that night, though, I am calm and the comfort washes over me. I'm covered in teenage boy smell and surrounded by dirty boxer briefs and I'm okay.

A little bit of me still imagines bits and pieces of it though. The pictures on her desk. A flash of red hair. Her inhumanly white teeth. Looking at anything but her eyes while I was there. It's like having a toothpick stab into me every time. A toothpick to my urethra. A toothpick to my clit. A toothpick, three, five, six, in my pussy. Hard. Hard. Hard. Push. Push. Push.

CHAPTER 9

ANGRY

—

That night, after Marshal's and toothpicks and teenage boy, I went to sleep slowly. I was half asleep at 1 AM and three-quarters asleep at 2 AM, but I didn't actually fall asleep until after 3 AM. And I woke up slowly too. In fact, I woke up so slowly that I slept through school lunch. And then I got out of bed and, during my walk from my (now bleach-scented) bedroom to the living room, decided that I wouldn't be going to school at all that day. Only one more class. What would the point of it be?

Part of me wanted to find my mom or Jen or Brigham sitting at the kitchen table when I reached it. But mom was still at work. Jen was still at college, probably totally oblivious to it all. And maybe Brigham was at work... But what if he was like me today?

Maybe he wouldn't feel the toothpicks in his balls like I did, but maybe getting ready for college next year has become a waste to him, too.

An hour later I get a call on the landline. It's Brigham's voice. "Lacey? Hey, you didn't come to school today. What happened? I've been waiting to pick you up for like fifteen minutes!"

"Wait, am I really the only one that couldn't get up this morning? What the fuck? I must be crazy." And, of course, college is still important to Brigham. It's the only way for him to get out of his dad's house, to get away from the memories of his brother, to get out of Pennyworth and closer to the hospital that cared enough to save him. He's moving on. Why can't I?

"Why couldn't you get up this morning? Everything seemed to be going really well with Marshal last night. Was it because Weedo had to go inside?"

"I mean, maybe. But--"

"Matthews, the police is doing all that they can for all of this. You gotta focus on school okay? It's the only way that either of us are ever getting out of here alive." He hinders on the last word like it's stuck in his throat. Of course, he's still stuck on losing Donte and the hospital. How could he not be? But if he's stuck on that stuff, and I'm stuck on Rosalyn, how the fuck am I supposed to know which one to focus on? It's not like his losing his brother is unimportant. It's not like his landing in the hospital because of it is something to be taken lightly. But I've been bleeding out of my pussy the last several days, and I'm not even on my fucking period. It physically hurts.

"Blue, hey."

"What?", he sounds pissed off at me.

"I know that college is really important to the both of us. And I know that we both have a lot of shit that we're dealing with right now. Never, for the love of fucking god, tell me to focus on school when I've been fucking fucked, and it fucking hurt like mother fucking hell."

"Wait, how can you possibly be pissed at me?"

"No one close to you expected you to just go back to work right away after you wound up in the hospital. Even your boss was surprised, and all that he knew was that you were in the hospital. He didn't even know what for."

"What's your point?"

"I'm not you, okay? I'm not completely there yet. Maybe you think that I should be acting normally, but I can't function like my life is normal yet. I'm not even so sure if your working so quickly is quite you. It might just be the fear that your dad will fucking yell at you if you sit around at home."

"There's no "just the fear" that he'll yell at me. That's a big fucking deal and you have to know that. The fuck, Matthews. Your mom doesn't yell at you for none of your shit."

But why would she? I'm me. She has no reason to ask me about school. She knows that I live the chink's lifestyle, that I always have, and I almost certainly always will. That only slightly changed when Blue wound up in the hospital, and my grades have been solid since then. Nothing happens during senior year of high school. If I were anything but a chink no one would yell at me to be the model minority I have always been destined to be. It's almost too much for me to hear everything that Brigham is spitting into my ear over the phone. Or, actually, it is too much.

"Why the fuck would she yell at me? She knows that I'm one of the model fucking minority in this town! Everyone calls me a chink, and everyone tells you that I live the chink's lifestyle! I'm not perfect because I want to be, Brigham Blue! I'm fucking perfect because I fucking have to be! And now I've been fucking raped! We both have it fucking bad!"

Before he even has the opportunity to respond, I slam the phone into its landline dock. And the house is so quiet that it's loud. And I know that if I have to run into Brigham, he'll try to hug me or he'll try to punch me, and I'm not in the mood for either.

And then the phone rings again. How anticlimactic.

I don't even consider answering. I just jot down a note for my mom and leave it out on the kitchen table. "Woke up late today bc of R. Going to the beach. Be back b4 tomorrow morning. Love you."

I've never gone out on my own at night before. In Pennyworth it isn't really suggested, but my mom knows where I am, and no one really goes to the beach anymore. No one but me and Blue, and maybe some random stragglers every once in a while. I actually don't know if they used to go very often, like before I was born or anything. But, anyway, they don't do it presently.

How little I really know has been blaringly obvious to me for the majority of my life. I'm a senior in high school, and you'd expect the curriculum to get pretty damn close to what we actually need to know before we escape into the real world, but we don't learn much. We learn how to cram for tests, but we don't learn how to learn. We're taught to hate the things that are crammed down our spitty and sticky mouths and coughing throats.

The Asians are especially taught that we should stay up until odd hours of the night or else fail our families entirely. At least the chinks are. Maybe other Asians are different.

We're taught that everything is valued under college. Except maybe the academic pride of our families and their judgmental relatives. Even our friends. Even our brains. Even the things that we'd rather be doing. I'd like to be a writer someday. But my entire family screams at me to become a doctor or a nurse or an accountant or a lawyer, and wow look at all those choices I have. They all require me to go to school for at least eight years. Most of them for more than a decade. I'll be almost thirty by the time that I get out and finish running away from the expectations. But they'll still have succeeded. And I'll have lost my entire life doing things that I hate, missing out on people that I could've loved, or fucked, or loved and fucked.

Toothpick.

Something else.

Move on.

Sunset.

By the time that I reach the beach I sneak my toes into the sand. I watch a dolphin breach. Can dolphins breach? I know that whales can. Yeah, why not. I fucking saw a dolphin breach.

Everywhere else in town there are cigarette butts and bits and pieces of trash that no one bothers to clear from the sidewalks, but there's almost nothing here. I don't even see any kids here. I don't see any beach balls. I don't see any remnants of a sandcastle. But I see an overturned umbrella. And for a moment I tempt myself with the metaphorical significance of an umbrella stuck wrong side up on a random patch of sand, how maybe it means that my life has also turned upside down because someone left me in the middle of something when they weren't meant to. *Too poetic? Too poetic.*

By the time that I reach the umbrella I've somehow, unconsciously made the decision to pick it up. When I finally realize that I've gotten it in my hands, I can't decide if I want to stand it back up or somehow bring it home with me. What time is it now? Maybe 3:30 PM? Maybe 4? I have at most twelve hours to decide what to do with it. If I decide that it's somehow important, I'll grab it later. I'll stick it right side up for now. *Toothpick. Something else. Move on.* I'm two feet from the water.

I don't fight with people very often, but clearly something happened that made me snap. Maybe I should be madder in general, or maybe that's how people would be living if Pennyworth were a little more ideal in the emotions department. How many people does it take to convince an entire town that emotions are this fucking shameful?

Everyone must know that everyone else is hurting, right?

Or, maybe, the truth is that most people don't really know. They probably hear everyone that they know telling them to keep their chins up and then see most people doing exactly that. They probably don't care to notice that they say the same thing to everybody else, that they tell everyone the same bullshit that they've been told their entire lives.

Chin up.

Toothpick?

Chin up.

Dead father?

Chin up.

Lost brother?

Chin up.

Best friend attempted suicide?

Chin up.

Sister away in college?

Chin up.

Best friend doesn't really seem to care about any of this?

Chin up.

Or maybe he's pulling off the act that he's expected to pull off. Maybe he sees everyone else with their chins held high and doesn't know that he's totally justified to act the way that he has. Maybe he's one of the people who doesn't know that everyone cries, at least every once in a while. Maybe he's forgetting that most of the people in this town have lost something really valuable: they aren't allowed to feel, the racists have taken away their families, they don't have the freedom to live in the peace that they deserve, their mayor is doing everything he can to ensure that.

But, if he doesn't know that, what does he make of me? Maybe I'm the crazy exception that he finally got to know, and now that he knows I'm the exception, it's time to skip out on me.

It's eight o'clock when I let my stomach win out. Of course, the water is piss warm at night and I can barely let myself leave behind a small sand tower that I've made. I've been wading for hours, just thinking of the same things over and over again. Mostly about Brigham and where he might be. Partly about toothpicks, and how the toothpicks probably won't end for several months. And what if I don't want to press charges, just because it hurts so much? Is it too late to pull back the police report?

By the time I make it back to the umbrella, I've decided to leave it behind. It looks too much like a giant toothpick to me, now that I see it. In the afternoon, this umbrella was me, and I helped it back onto it's right-side-up. But now that it's evening, it doesn't feel like me at all. A metaphorical umbrella rotation doesn't mean that my mood is gonna turn around, and now that it's doing the simple job it's meant to do, I can't relate to the struggle I thought it was having before. But it wasn't struggling.

This is an umbrella: A plastic stick and a plastic sheet standing up to make shade for a nonexistent family that left it behind.

This isn't Lacey Matthews.

This is an umbrella.

Toothpick.

Part of me starts getting this stirring feeling in my chest of wanting to run. And I don't really want to run anywhere in particular, I just don't want to go home. But I go home anyway, I don't listen to the stirring. I know that if I do, I'll end up outside of the Cliffords' house, or outside of Blue's house, or I'll go to the diner just to see if he's working tonight. He will be working there tonight. And if not, maybe he's in therapy right now.

At home I find my mom at the kitchen table, smiling a little sadly. I don't know that I've ever seen that look on her face before, not even at dad's funeral. "Lacey, I got your note when I came back from work", she told me.

"Sorry about that, Mama, I'll be going back to school tomorrow. Today was a little…", I have to take a moment to think, "unplanned."

"Don't worry, I understand why you'd want to go. My goodness, you put more pressure on yourself than I ever could. I blame your father. It's his fault that my family thinks I'm so soft on you."

"Heh, you're right, Mama. How was work?"

"After school I picked up someone's shift at the ReadyMart. It was fine, I think. I made a little bit extra, so maybe the two of us can go out sometime this weekend." Sometimes I forget about all the jobs she has to juggle. "I'll splurge a little and we can get a meal at the diner together. Maybe we can invite Brigham?"

"No, Mama, I'd really like it if it were just the two of us. Let's do it when we know he isn't working, okay? I'm taking a lot of this stuff really hard, and we kinda had a fight today." I'm glad that he was there to tell her about the rape stuff happening so that I didn't have to, but I have to be pissed about what he expected of me earlier this afternoon.

"Then I won't say another word about that tonight," she does a cute little chuckle there, "I got home around six, and I had some dinner without you. If you like, I can heat something up and sit with you. I've been working a lot lately, huh? And when I get home, you're in your room working, so we've hardly seen each other." I'm so relieved that she doesn't push me to talk about anything tonight.

"Dinner sounds amazing, Mama, thank you."

CHAPTER 10

CHIN UP

———

As soon as I finished dinner with my mom, I started research-
ing ways to deal with depression under the guise that I was
looking for ways to help Blue. But I think that this is also
possible, I might've also been looking for myself. All I have
really is an old Psychology Textbook the Psych teacher let
me keep. It must've been after they got in a new shipment,
so it's older and not the most updated. But it's what I have.

After Rosalyn finger fucked me, after reporting to the
police about Rosalyn fucking raping me, after watching my
best friend attempt suicide, I think that my brain was tired.

The most commonly heard of ways to get over depression are therapy and drugs, and then there are those suicide
hotlines that I've seen in the phonebook before. I know that
my single mother doesn't have the money to spend a couple
hundred extra dollars a week for me to talk to any of the

sucky therapists in town, or to pay for a psychiatrist and any prescribed drugs, and definitely not enough for if the worst happened and I had to be admitted to a hospital anywhere. And suicide hotlines are for people who wanna die real bad and who have plans and shit.

Right now, I don't think that I want to die. But I kinda just don't wanna experience more life right now, especially if it keeps going so downhill. I know that I'm a senior in high school and so the workload isn't really that bad, but even the little work that I have to do is looking more and more like a mountain of things that are unattainable or unfinishable or just un-able-to-do-able.

I am unable.

I am unable do the simple Spanish homework where I change verbs into other forms of verbs.

I am unable to draw a simple line on a graph for my Statistics homework.

I am unable to avoid getting drunk after more than half a pint of beer.

I am unable to avoid getting finger fucked by some weak-ass girl that scared me shitless in the morning.

I am unable to keep my best friend from wanting to die all the time. I am unable to do anything at all.

I am even unable to will myself guts enough to actually take action on everything that's happened, like Blue has done.

I am unable to stop being mad at the only person that has actively helped me with any part of this rape shit.

I think that last one is the one that makes me feel the most sick.

Unless things get bad enough, I won't get any help at all, or I'll have to find some way to give a fuck ton of money that I don't have to a person that I don't know. I could always pretend to make things look worse than they are, but then Blue hasn't done that either. My brain is so tired. Maybe I should get Blue to do that. Maybe I should find a way to stop being so mad at Blue. All he tried to do was care about me. All he did was try to encourage me to continue business as normal even when life isn't so normal.

I've been raped.

But who cares?

Wheaton doesn't.

"Chin up".

My classmates never would.

"Chin up".

Blue?

I mean he practically told me to keep my chin up this afternoon.

"Keep your chin up".

I don't know how to go about this. I know that he wants what's best for me. But I also know that he doesn't really know everything that I've been experiencing. He doesn't know how much I feel like my body has betrayed me in not fighting Rosalyn harder. In not yelling at her louder. In not being good enough at being at least a little sober. This feels like my body's fault. *Is it my fault? Is it really Rosalyn's?* She seemed so certain that I never said anything. But I only remember that morning that everything happened. I don't remember the night before at all. She said that I never said anything. Maybe I never said anything. But didn't I say stuff in the morning? I don't even remember much of that anymore. I mostly remember flashes of what happened, I remember the idea of pain, and I remember running through the house to find pants.

I remember a picture too. *Was that really my dad? Couldn't be. But it was.*

A lot of me is just so exhausted with every fucking thought that I have, and I can't stand up straight enough anymore. Before I can even start to think any more about pictures or pants or blood, I hear a tinkling sound. It's coming from outside, so I cautiously walk over to the window, just in case the police are doing something shitty at this hour of the night. But, when I peel back the lavender curtain, it's just Blue, his soft knuckles making contact over and over with the windowpane. The sound reminds me of fairy dust in those little kid movies, so much so that the magic of it takes over a little bit and I forget that I'm pissed at him. But I only forget for a microsecond.

I almost throw the curtains closed in his face.

Almost.

He wouldn't be here if it weren't something important. I'm just hoping that that something comes with an apology at some point.

I jerk my head in the direction of the front door, motioning that I'll let him in if he comes around. And he hurries. I'm glad that he hurries, even though I am mad. Only fireworks tonight, if I can help it. When he makes it to the front door I've only been there for a half-moment. I open the door and let him in almost silently. Almost immediately I get wrapped in a massive Blue bear hug.

"Lacey, I'm so fucking sorry. I know you're pissed at me. Y'know I just want you to do well in school. But, god, I just don't know anything about how to deal with that shit. I fucking hate that my best friend got hurt and I wasn't there to help her."

"You were there when I called though. Right after Rosalyn literally fucked me up, you came over like a madman and made sure I was okay. You did everything that you could have that day. But...," I nail him in the shoulder, "I'm pissed that you expected me to deal with that shit so fast. What the fuck, dude?"

"I think I've been too focused on that lately. But it's good that you're doing a little better already. It's good that I have something to focus on after Donte," by now he's started to tear up, "But I think I've gotten really focused on the idea that I have to be doing well, that I have to look like I'm doing okay. I'm spending too much fucking time trying so hard not to think about my brother. I'm spending too much fucking time trying not to think about some trashy chick hurting my best friend. But when you try not to think about things, you end up not being able to think about anything else. And it all just makes me wish it would all go away, that this is my--"

He has to take a deep breath. Through that entire speech he doesn't make a pause, he just stumbles from one word to the next with so much speed and desperation. It's like he has to stop himself before he gives up everything inside, the things he's afraid to admit to even his best friend.

"Blue," I start to say. He looks up at me in the middle of his breath, so it's almost like I've picked up talking when he no longer can. "This isn't your fault. What Donte did isn't your fault. Rosalyn being a shitty human isn't your fault. And you being sad about everything that's going on–well your emotions aren't quite something you can control, y'know?"

"Lace..." His thought collides with his need to sweep me into a hug again. He holds me like he's afraid he's got something to lose. But, maybe the truth of the matter is that he's holding on tight to something so that he doesn't lose himself. "Eh ehe, thank you for forgiving me. I don't deserve it. Shit."

Outside we hear a couple fireworks and Weedo yelling at them to get out of his face. One of the policemen shouts a couple homophobic slurs before finally backing off.

Before he has the opportunity to even ask, I let him know, "I don't think it's safe for you to go out right now." I laugh to myself a little nervously. "You can stay here tonight. You take the bed; I can grab the couch or sleep in my mom's room. Only fireworks tonight."

I say all of this and he hasn't even let go of the hug yet, although the hold has loosened some. I feel him nod softly into my neck, and it's only at that point that I also feel that several tears have gathered there. I only notice when he spreads the wetness around. The skin at my right shoulder gets slightly colder.

"Thanks, Lacey." He lets go and smiles at me, a little ashamedly and a little gratefully, both.

"Lacey," he starts to speak as he lets go of me, "There's a couple things that I need to tell you. I should've told you about it sooner, but the whole thing with Rosalyn happened and that felt more important."

"Okay, what is it?" I'm suddenly impatient.

"Can we go to your room? I don't want your mom to hear."

"Sure, Blue." And I lead the way to my room like he hasn't been to my house before, like we're both walking into some foreign territory and I don't know what I'm doing.

When we get to my room he sits on the side of my bed, and I sit beside him. He looks like he's holding his breath, and clearly, he's anxious to tell me what's happening. He keeps opening his mouth to start talking and then swallowing hard, like he's physically trying to keep the words from coming out of his mouth. He keeps tracing the lilac patterning on my comforter, and I don't know if I've ever seen him nervous enough to do anything like that before.

"Blue? Hey, what's up?" I have to speak after he starts to look out the window. Has he forgotten what he needs to say?

"Do you remember why we went to the bar?"

"No, I don't. I only remember them inviting us and then us showing up. I figured that there was some motive to it, but I didn't know what. By the time that we got there, they just said that they needed you. I thought it was sexist, and I probably would've done well to say something about it, but they only talked to you. I sat down and talked to Rosalyn."

"Right, right." He cringes when I say her name. "I'm sorry about that, again," he tells me before giving me a quick squeeze of a hug.

I have to shrug him off to encourage him to keep going, "So what happened? What're you gonna tell me?"

"Right. They wanted me to tell them how to get to the top of the highest building. They told me that if I didn't, they would go to the school and report you for being on restricted property. And they also told me that they would report me to the police. You would've probably been arrested and sent to juvie or something, for at least a little while. I would've probably had to get bail paid or spend some time in jail. It wouldn't be bad enough to get me sent to prison, but we both would've had stuff on our records."

"Wait what? When are they gonna report us? Can we lie our way out of it? There has to be something we can do."

"I agreed to tell them how to get up there."

"Wait what?" I say again. I'm taken aback, "Why would you tell them that? They have no business up there. Why didn't you talk to me?"

"I didn't wanna get in your way. You don't need that kinda shit on your records. That doesn't gotta show up when you're applying to colleges. I knew that if I told you, you wouldn't let me do it. I mean, it's kinda a place with not-so-good memories attached to it."

"I need you to stop telling me that you're getting in my way. You're not in my way. I've already told you that you're one of the only people that cares enough to help me." Deep breath. I don't know when, but I've started to tear up again. "Did you tell them already?"

"Yeah, I did, back at the bar when you were with Rosalyn," he gets quiet for a moment when he mentions her name, "But they haven't tried it yet. They want me to show them how to do it first. I was supposed to go back to the bar later. They want me to walk there with them."

"What do they even want with it?"

"My guess is that Wood and Nail have both wanted it for a really long time. It's some gang territory symbol they want. I don't know enough now."

"Why would Nail even need it? Those racist assholes are all white except for the people that've gotten some dirty work done for them. If I had to choose between them, I'd pick Wood."

"You don't know either of them, Lace. On what grounds would you even be picking them?"

"I don't know. They're less racist, anyway. And if I could actually pick, I wouldn't pick anyone at all."

"But we don't get to pick. I've already told them, and I'm sorry about that. I have to show them. As soon as I get out of here, I have to get back there. I picked up our fakes from Marshal before I came over to talk to you."

"Why would you get both of them? I don't wanna go back there. What if Rosalyn's there?"

"We already paid for them, Lace. You might as well take it." He practically shoves the plastic into my hand. "And besides, I want you to be there. Last time I let them really corner me and you didn't know what was going on until less than an hour ago."

I trace the edges of the fake id with my left pointer finger. I have to think for a while before I answer. *If I go, what if she's there? I couldn't face her again,* one part of my brain thought. Another thought, *but he needs you. You should do it.* The second one won out.

"Okay, I'll go with you. I've got your back, Blue." And I have to let out a smile because it's Blue I'm talking to.

In less than twenty minutes I'm wearing jeans and sitting on his handlebars. The police left the area almost an hour ago, but my heart still feels like it's fighting to get out of my chest. I'm not religious, but I start to pray that we won't run into anyone on the way to the bar. And we do run into one person, but he's drunk and attempting to make his way home. He even waves as we go by. And I wave back.

We reach the bar more quickly than I expect us to, and I don't really calm down for a while. As soon as we walk in, I see some of the members from Nail that were here last time. Weedo is here. Marshal is here. Thompson is here. A few others that I don't know by name, but I vaguely recognize.

They're mostly incapacitated or just generally really drunk. Weedo's kinda high, but he can still hold a semi-intelligent conversation.

"Hey, what's happening tonight, exactly?"

"Oh. Hey, Matthews! I didn't know you were coming." Clearly Weedo's surprised to see me here with Blue.

"Yeah, Brigham invited me. And I already have my fake so I might as well use it, right?"

"Ah hah, yeah. Makes sense to me. But I don't know how long we're gonna stay here. Brigham tell you we're going to the tallest building tonight? He says he's gonna show us how to get up there."

"He told me, yeah. But I don't know if it's a good idea to get you guys up there. What do you even want in that place?"

"Well, we don't want Wood to have it. It's got a great vantage point over that area of the city, and territory is territory, y'know? It'd be good for us. It'd show everyone in Wood what their place is."

"What's their place?"

"They just aren't better than we are. We're stronger and better."

I think to myself and compare the two groups in my head. Nail is mostly white men. A sprinkle of color where, I guess, they see fit. I don't know if I saw much of anything besides men. My dad was in Nail. There are only guys here tonight.

And Wood is, as far as Blue has told me, everyone else in between. If either of us were to be let into one of them, it would be Wood. He said there are girls in the group all the time, even a few Asian ones. It isn't only men.

It makes me wonder if that's why Weedo is so desperate to keep anyone from finding out he and Marshal are together. He's in need of a leg up, and he's willing to lie for it. He's even roped Marshal into lying for it, for him.

Half a moment later I see a flash of red hair. "Hey, Weedo, I'll talk to you later. Don't let anyone leave without me."

Earlier I was set on never seeing her again, and part of me definitely thought about hiding so that she wouldn't see me here at all. But something in me makes me walk up to her, want to demand answers. Not about her fingering me, about something else.

"What do you know about John Matthews?" I don't even give her time to notice me before I speak. She turns around like she's reacting to a loud noise, not like she's recognized a voice.

She gasps when she sees me. I watch the image of my face click into place in her brain. I don't think she's even heard the question. She just stands up and meets me.

"I didn't think I'd see you again." She's nervous. Her hair is down and she's wearing a loose-fitting white top and light-wash denim jeans. She grabs a tendril of her hair and starts to wrap it around her fingers, subconsciously it looks like. "What are you doing here?"

"Did you know John Matthews?" I ignore her questions, and I ask again. "There was a picture in your sister's room of him. His arm was wrapped around your mom."

"Yeah, I knew him. He died a while ago, didn't he? He was my mom's boyfriend for a while."

"He wasn't your dad?"

"No, and I'm glad for that. He tried to act like he was my dad, though. He tried to play with me like I was his kid or something, for a while. Eventually he gave up."

"Did he die when he and your mom were still together?"

"Yeah, I think so. My mom cried a lot when it happened, I remember. We went to his funeral, I think." She pauses for a moment before asking me a question, "Wait why do you care about him?"

"He was my father. He died because he was sneaking out of my house to go and see your mom. That was almost a decade ago."

And now she's really quiet. I think I might've somehow managed to show her too much about myself.

She looks like she's going to apologize, but I turn on my heel before she can say anything. I never want to see her again. I finally know what I've always wanted to know about my father. And I feel sick about it.

Of course he fell in love with Gracie. She has a connection outside of town. She knows how to feel. And she's kind—just look at how well she took care of Blue.

And, luckily, Rosalyn isn't his kid. Not a single tinge of bad would be in her body if she were.

I don't know why it feels important, but I also realize that I might've actually been my dad's last kid.

The conversation we had was short, but there are a lot of emotions to sift through.

Before I walk out, I'm tempted to tell Blue to show Nail the way up without me. But, before I get the chance to say anything, Thompson, who is stark sober, rushes over and tells us that they're calling it off for the night. "When Brigham said that there would be climbing involved, I thought it might be better to do this on a night when everyone's a little more..." he pauses to think of the right phrasing, "a little more in their right minds."

And so I've left the bar without a single sip of alcohol passing through my lips. But, oddly enough, my thoughts leave me feeling just as foggy.

For a few days, after I'd talked to Rosalyn, after I'd found out about my dad's relationship with her mom, I couldn't think straight. I remember the stuff that I have to remember, but not much else. At some point, while I was in the mist, I remember there was a phone call.

I only remember fragments of it. It was with Blue.

"Lacey, I think that you should go back to school soon. You haven't been in over a week."

"Why should I bother? It's senior year. There's nothing going on."

"You're gonna fuck up your grades, Lace."

"I can't fuck up my grades this way. Not enough is happening. Not that it even matters if I'm just going to community college after this. There truly isn't a better time for my life to fall apart."

"What the fuck are you talking about?"

"If my life falls apart now, it won't affect anything. That's the only silver lining I've got on this."

I don't remember much more than that. I remember me crying some. I think he yelled at me. Something about how he wishes he could break down. It was like a half-yell-half-cry.

He must've convinced me to go back to school at some point during that call. I have no other significant events to recollect any kind of timeline. I mean, maybe I decided on my own, but I can't imagine doing that. I don't remember doing that.

The only reason I say that he must've convinced me is because there was suddenly a day, it must've been a Monday, where I woke up and I got out of bed. I felt obligated to climb out of bed and to take a shower and put on clean clothes. I robotically ate a breakfast bar. I robotically slung my backpack onto my right shoulder. I robotically open the front door and lock it behind me. I robotically turn right, cross the street at the corner, turn right again, turn left, cross the street, turn left again, turn right...

I get to school in less than twenty minutes, on autopilot. I am exactly two minutes early to my first class, just like I always am. Just like I used to be, I mean.

I keep my head down whenever I see Weedo or Marshal or Thompson. I keep my head down whenever I see anyone white. I just instinctively think that they're all from Nail, and I don't need them to see me. I don't need to see them. Best to stay out of their way.

It's been two weeks. And I've stayed on autopilot for most of the time. I cry when I'm at home, but I don't like letting myself do that. I don't like letting myself think about everything. I'd rather bottle it up, starve it of oxygen, hope that it dies, and I can just move on. Admittedly, I cry two or three times a day. I don't know what to do about any of it. Nothing has been good, and it feels impossible to rectify. The possibility that I'm depressed dawns on me. I try to bottle it up. Chin up.

CHAPTER 11

TALK

Have you ever had someone run straight at you, just totally out of nowhere? My answer to that question used to be no, but Thompson had other ideas, I guess. Let me tell you, being head butted in the stomach fucking hurts like hell. And he somehow managed to head butt me while also wrapping his red-hoodied-arms really tight around my chest. It isn't like my boobs are that big or anything, but still. I swear he tried his hardest to get his hands to touch his elbows.

I don't remember hitting the ground, but I do remember launching my body off it. I remember very few words, but my mind went into autopilot again. A different kind of autopilot though.

There was so much adrenaline, and my vision sharpened, and I was so pissed.

I recall things being said. But everything was so blurry, I didn't hear anything.

I also don't remember doing anything in order to unwrap his body from mine, but he's on his knees and gripping his head for a couple of moments. There's a dull *thud-thud-thud* in my left shoulder. I'll probably bruise there later.

He tries to punch me a couple of times, but I maneuver my body out of the way.

We both try to take each other down onto the ground, but we're too on guard to even allow ourselves to touch each other, to allow the other to even brush us. That is until I somehow manage to elbow him in the chest before I hear whistles in the background.

There's shouting.

I get caught off guard, but he must have kept going without thinking. He runs at me again. Another head butt. He's on top of me. I see him start to raise his head up from the floor like he's going to hit me in the head with it.

He doesn't get the chance to though.

I freeze when I hear extra loud footsteps echoing across the hallway, and right before he gets to slam his face down onto me, there's another body that pulls his body off my body.

The principle lets me off with a warning. He lets me know that I can go home. However, he drags Thompson off to his office. I know for a fact that he's done this before. He's done worse before. This isn't new. This is protocol.

But why me?

He's never hated me before. I haven't even done any-thing wrong. When we were at the bar, Thompson was the one who told me that we were going to wait before we went to the tallest building again. Has he gone impatient? Did Blue talk to him about something that I don't know about? Was he drunk? Is that what it is? Is he just an angry drunk?

Whatever. I'm going home.

I guess I haven't ever gone home during the middle of school because I'm starting to look at my surroundings like they're something totally different. The streets are unrecog-nizable when there aren't any people in them. The trees are different colors in this light. They're a bit more of a brighter green, I think. I've rarely been outside at this time, ever, and it's quiet. It's not eerily quiet. It's a calm quiet.

I haven't broken a smile out of real happiness in a few weeks, but I almost do. I start to feel hopeful now.

I don't think it's because I'm out of school early. But it is nice to think about being home when that's all I've really wanted to do since Blue convinced me to go back to school. I know that he wants me there, but it feels like a small victory that I've been told to go home. Or did the principle just say that I could go home? Whatever, I should listen to the guy that runs the school, right?

I'm expecting the streets to be pretty quiet, but I'm sur-prised. When I'm walking back home, I see Sadie. Sadie Clif-ford. From the coffee shop. Sadie Clifford. Gracie Clifford's daughter. Sadie Clifford. The girl who gave me clothes when mine got ruined after Blue's suicide attempt. Sadie Clifford. The older sister of Rosalyn Clifford, the girl who assaulted me. Sadie Clifford.

Before I connect all the dots and get to that last one, my hand waves at her all on its own. I flash a quick, fake smile at her and tilt my head to my right. Why am I trying so hard to make it look like I'm excited to see her?

"Hey, Lacey. How've you been doing? Long time no see." I can tell that she knows what Rosalyn did. Her voice is too concerned, like she's trying to be a big sister to me. Why isn't she on Rosalyn's side?

"Hi, Sadie. I've been..." I feel like I can't tell her that I've been doing well. "I've been better." I laugh a little half sigh of a pity laugh.

"Yeah, I bet. I'm sorry."

"It's okay... Actually it's not okay. But it will be."

"I'm glad that at least you know it'll be alright eventually, and it will be." There's a moment of silence before she speaks again. I notice a bird come down onto the sidewalk and peck at a little bit of grass. "I'm just getting back from running some errands, and I've got some time before I have to head out of Pennyworth again. Did you wanna catch up at all? We could talk."

The bird has a stick in its beak now. I watch it fly up into a nearby tree and see a bunch of sticks already piled up into some small semblance of a nest. "Yeah, I'd like that."

This spot is closer to the Cliffords' house than it is to mine. Way closer actually. Funny that the bird decided to live here. "Where would you like to be? I know that my house is a little closer to here than yours, but I can understand if you don't wanna go back there. And you're obviously on your way back home anyway."

"I don't mind going back to yours. You've already walked all this way." I actually don't mind. Part of me just wants to look at that picture of my dad again. Another part of me is just happy to see Sadie, just because she was so kind to me before that I can't help but to trust her again now. And another part, still, kinda just wants to go back. It feels like things are unfinished there for some reason. "When do you go back to work?"

"Not until this evening. We've got hours! I know that if we talk it'll probably be hard stuff..." She looks at me a little apologetically, "But I also don't know if you can talk about it a whole bunch with anyone right now. Not a lot of people are willing to listen. Not everyone gets it either, y'know?"

"Wait, do you mean that something like this has happened to you too?"

She nods silently. "Back when I was still in high school. My first boyfriend— ehh heh— he acted pretty entitled about my body. Of course, if I had known any better, I wouldn't have let it go on for such a long time." She looks thoughtfully at the bird in its nest, and I follow my eyes in that direction. The bird doesn't mind being looked at. "I know that it's not quite the same as what you experienced, but there were so many times where I just wanted him to stop and just listen to me." Her vision breaks hold from the bird we've been watching, and she looks over at me. "But I know that Rose didn't really listen to you either."

"Rose?"

"Rosalyn."

"That's a nice nickname."

"Ehh heh, considering the circumstances, maybe I should use it less often. She doesn't really deserve me being so kind to her right now, does she?"

At this point we start walking over to her house, and everything feels familiar in a backwards sort of way. The only time that I was conscious and in this area, I was going the other way, I was running away, and then biking away. Now I'm walking back in.

When I get into her bedroom, it's like I'm seeing it for the first time. I didn't get a good look around the first time that I was in here and I was looking for jeans to borrow after Rosalyn had ruined my bottoms. It's still really nice, really prettily furnished, the wall color is a calm cream, the bed set is all soft blue, the blankets are velvety. The curtains match the bed spread, and so much light comes into the room at this time of the day.

And she has more pictures than what I initially only saw on her cork board set up. There are polaroids on strings of light on the wall, on her headboard, stuck in a couple of slits on her closet doors. It seems really nice. There are so many personal touches too: little ceramic pencil holders and stuffed animals on the bed and a guitar in the corner of the room by the window. And, would you believe it? she has a pet fish. I haven't seen anyone with a pet in Pennyworth since... I don't think I've seen anyone with a pet ever.

I make it a point to go to her cork board directly and to look at the picture of her and Rosalyn and my dad smiling together.

So he was happy here. And he loved them. I guess I'd always wondered that, always wanted to know.

"She told me that he was your dad." My body jerks when I hear her speak. I'd forgotten that another person was here, in the room, with me.

"He must've loved you guys a lot to come hang out with you all the time. Look at how happy he was here."

"I don't know if he was really that happy here, to be honest. I mean, he lived with you and your sister and your mom. He didn't live here."

"I know he didn't live here, but he worked so hard to make sure that I didn't know that you guys existed. He would sneak over here in the middle of the night to come visit. He didn't ever want me to see him leaving."

"He'd always leave here in broad daylight. I think he was very clear about where he felt like his place was. He wanted to get back to his own kid, I think. He talked about you all the time. Not really anyone else, actually. He'd really only talk about you."

"I didn't know that I'd had that much significance in his life. Why wouldn't he talk about any of his other kids?"

"Maybe you were the only one?"

"Heh. Maybe."

"I don't know a whole bunch about him, but it's obvious that he cared a lot about you. He was mostly here 'cause he was super into my mom, and I guess her having kids was a plus because he liked to play with us and give us attention too. But I don't think we were quite what he was expecting."

"Why do you say that?"

"He wanted to teach us how to do some martial arts stuff the first couple of times that he was visiting, but Rose and I weren't really into it. Must've been something that he taught you how to do, huh?"

"Yeah, I used to be really good. Or, at least, that was what he told me. I'm sure he was just being nice because I was a little kid. But I liked it a lot." I cross my arms and grab onto both of my elbows. It's been a long time since I've talked about this kind of thing with anybody besides Blue.

"You must've been really strong and fast, hm?"

"If I really were, I wouldn't have been stuck under Rosalyn for so long."

"Hey, you know that isn't true." Her first syllable is really harsh, but then her voice softens. And I know that she's right. I mean, she would know, right?

"Yeah, I know. It was like I just froze. I was so scared to make her angry or... I was just really surprised. I was caught so off guard. I mean, I'd just woken up, and then she was on top of me in the other room, and I froze, and when I came back to thinking I kept asking her what was happening and that she needed to stop, but I couldn't move like at all y'know? I could barely talk as much as I did." I didn't realize it, but in the middle of remembering I started crying, and Sadie started to wrap her arms around my body like she understood. Maybe she does understand.

"What she did isn't cool, and I hope that she pays for it. I'm really sorry that it happened to you."

"But she acted so genuinely surprised to see that she was hurting me. She thought we were roleplaying or something. What if she really didn't do anything wrong? She's a good person, right? What if it was my fault for not saying anything? I mean, I'm the one who got drunk. I'm the one who came home with her. I'm the one that decided to talk to a stranger when my friends were busy. It was my fault, right?"

"Hey, hey. That's not how this works."

"How do you know how it works? What do you even fucking mean? It's obviously my fault that I let this stuff happen. She was so certain that she was doing everything right. She won't admit that she was wrong, so maybe I'm the one that's wrong."

"She never asked you what you wanted. She heard you saying that you wanted to stop, and she didn't even stop to think that maybe you might mean it. In the off chance that you didn't mean it, sure it would've been a momentary mood-killer, but she didn't even think about it being a possibility that she needed to clarify." Now she unwraps herself from me and looks me straight in the face. "This is not your fault. You didn't want it and she didn't ask. You didn't tell her it was okay. This. Is. Not. Your. Fault. Lacey."

The last of those syllables pound extra hard into my brain. "So, if it isn't my fault, what do I do now?"

"You have to focus on healing. Just focus on surviving for now, until you feel like your body is yours again, until you feel like you can love yourself again, until you can trust people again. Take your time."

"I don't know if you've noticed, but that isn't really normal here. No one really talks about that stuff or thinks about that stuff ever. I don't know where to even start doing any of that. And I have a whole bunch of other shit that I have to deal with on top of that. I've got Nail on my back. I've got my best friend to worry about. I have to focus on getting out of here somehow—"

"Whoa, whoa. Breathe." I guess I had a hard time stopping. It all tumbled out of me so quickly. "That's a lot to think about, but you've also got me to help you if you need it. And you have other friends it sounds like, and I'm sure that they're there to support you. It's a lot, I agree. But you aren't doing it alone."

At this point I just collapse. I fall on the floor, which is a *very* soft cream colored carpet by the way. I just cry at her feet until she crouches down next to me. And she holds me. And she keeps telling me that it'll be okay. And she says that it isn't my fault. And she strokes my hair. And I finally start to feel safe again, like actually safe, in the house of my rapist, after a fight in the middle of the day at school, in the middle of all of the Nail bullshit that Blue and I have to carry. It's odd.

"Thank you, Sadie. This means a lot. Thank you. And I'm sorry."

"Sorry for what?"

"I know that you're busy and you probably don't have a whole bunch of time for me right now. I'm sorry that I'm a lot."

"Hey, I made myself free for you today. I *wanted* to talk to you. I *chose* to talk to you. You aren't a lot. You're a person who's in pain and you're *allowed* to be."

By the time that I leave Sadie's, I've managed to stop crying and am able to peel myself off the floor. I wasn't expecting that at all, especially right after Thompson decided to fight me.

I still don't know what I did, or maybe if Blue did something, but clearly someone from Nail is mad with one or both of us if Thompson wanted to run at me like that. Did we wait too long to show them how to get up to the top of the tallest building? I know that they think it's an asset, that it's something that Nail and Wood have sought after for years and years, but I still think that it's quite arbitrary unless they're actually trying to cause mass destruction on that area of Pennyworth. But there's nothing of interest over there. I'm pretty sure that they both want it just because it isn't easily accessible, and probably one of them wants it just because the other one thought about wanting it first. Like I said, it seems pretty arbitrary.

I'm also still kinda freshly astounded at the fact that Sadie was able to cross paths with me like that when I needed it. I mean, it was like I didn't know how badly I needed to talk about it until I was actually given permission to talk about it. I just thought that I would deal with it like I normally deal with anything else. And I know that I've talked about it with Blue before, but that was mostly just a consequence of him being the person who helped me get out of the Cliffords' house the first time, after Rosalyn basically kidnapped and fucked me (literally) over. I think that, if he weren't there, maybe he wouldn't know about it at all. Probably no one would know about it at all. I probably wouldn't have let Blue tell my mom anything either, honestly. I mean, that's obvious. If I didn't tell him what happened there's no way that he could've told my mom. I wonder what that conversation was like...

I'm also just kinda shocked that something like what Rosalyn did to me could've happened to Sadie in the first place. I mean, she seems like she's too smart for it. But she did say that it went on for a long time. Some fuckers are really manipulative bitches, I guess. I don't even think that Sadie being smart could've had anything to do with it, with that being considered. The guy probably just took advantage of her because she trusted him. I mean, if I didn't think that I could trust Rosalyn at least a little bit when we first met, I probably wouldn't have wound up in her house.

Part of that makes me tempted to say that it was all my fault all over again, but Sadie was very clear about everything that she said. I mean, I didn't choose to get fucked. I wasn't asked to do anything, right? I wasn't even expecting to get that wasted.

On the way back home I see the spot where Sadie and I met up earlier this afternoon. It's been hours since then. But the sun still has some height in the sky. Sadie was starting to get ready to leave for work again when I said goodbye to her.

I look up into the tree again to see if the nest is still there and to see if the bird is still hanging out. The bird is still there, but it looks like the nest is missing. With another cursory look at the ground, I can see that someone has deliberately knocked it down. It's still kind of holding itself together, but there are lots of small pieces and an outline of a single dusty footprint going over it. Fuck.

I take the mostly whole piece in my hand and see how it holds up, and it kind of stays together. A couple small pieces fall off, but when I apply a little pressure to the top of it, it holds itself up. I tip toe and try to get the nest onto a higher branch than the first one, into a little tuft of leaves that'll make it a little more hidden. When I remember that I'm pretty small, I try hoist myself up a little higher on the tree with one of the lower lying branches. I put my foot into a little, natural notch near the base of the trunk. I put the nest where I think it'll make more sense, and I actually nestle it in pretty securely.

At one point I think that I must've scared the bird away without noticing. It's gone when I look for it again. I hope that it chooses to come back.

By the time that I get back to my house there's a letter in my mailbox, addressed to me. There's also a note on the fridge and two voicemails on the answering machine. I read the letter, written on official looking paper, and I see that my case won't be reviewed further. Rosalyn must've lied her ass off at the preliminary hearing.

Afterward I read the note that my mom left behind. Apparently, there was a last minute conference thing out of town and she had just enough time to hurry home, pack a couple of overnight things, and let me know.

Then I listen to the first voicemail. "This is a message for Lacey Matthews." I think that it's Mr. Smith's voice. "I'm just calling to let you know that I'm really sorry about the case falling through on you. You had so much evidence, but the camera that was provided wound up being compromised. There wasn't enough evidence without it. If you'd like to see if there's anything else we can do about this, please just give me a direct call. My personal number is..."

I jot down the number, just in case I decide that I actually want to try again. He goes on for a little bit longer about how the other officers probably wouldn't try to be as helpful with the case, how very sorry he is, blah, blah, blah. *Who the fuck did that to my photo evidence?* I delete the message when Mister finishes. I probably won't try again. With no evidence, I won't have anything stacked in my favor anyway. Oh well. Oh fucking well.

The second voicemail comes up automatically when I delete the first one. It's Blue's voice. "Hey, Lace. I didn't get the chance to tell you anything before it happened, and I'm so so sorry about it. A bunch of guys who said they were from Nail wound up in my neighborhood specifically looking for me. I didn't even recognize any of them, but they made me take them to the tallest building today and show them how to get to the top. Like they legit held me at gunpoint and forced me there. I was gonna tell you after school got out, but you weren't there when I tried to pick you up. And then I came to your house to see if you or your mom were here, but you obviously aren't, ehh heh. Call me back or something when you get back to your house and you hear this. I'm worried about you. And, uhh, yeah. I thought you needed to know. I'm sorry I couldn't tell you sooner. I'm sorry."

Okay, cool. Talk about a lot happening in one day.

I have to sit down and process some of this shit before I can actually figure out what I should be doing next. I mean, holy fuck. I knew there were a lot of hours in the day, but talk about an emotional roller coaster.

I can deal with a fight, especially if I'm the one who obviously won out in that situation. I can deal with a little bit of clarity from a really fucking cool conversation with Sadie. I was even starting to expect the court case to not go through because the when the fuck does a charge for rape actually work out in the victim's favor? And I guess I should've just expected the thing with Nail to have gone through eventually. I was mostly just ready for it to be done and over with. I should be pretty calm about it, but for some reason it's making me really stressed. I mean, they held my best friend at fucking gunpoint. And it's good that he's not anymore, but he was still being held at gunpoint and forced to do shit against his will.

I can deal with all that shit in pieces, but why the hell did it happen all in one day? Holy fuck. I have to call Blue.

I suddenly feel my body snap into action, like it's an emergency. I have to call Blue. I need to make sure that he's okay. I need to tell him that I'm okay. I need to tell him all the shit that happened to me today.

He picks up on the first ring. "Hello?"

"Hey, Blue. Sorry I just got home. I got your message."

"Holy fuck, Lace. You need to get a cell phone soon. Where've you been?"

"I was at the Cliffords'—"

"What the fuck were you doing back there? Are you okay? Did Rosalyn try to pull something else?"

"Oh, god no. Everything is fine. I ran into her sister, Sadie, on the way back home from school. The two of us talked for a while about what Rosalyn did. Trust me, Rosalyn never set foot in the house. It made me feel a lot better."

"What do you mean you guys talked about it? Even we haven't really talked about it. Weren't you afraid she would judge you or something?"

"No. I mean, at first, I was. But she told me that she dealt with some stuff like that too a while back. The only reason I felt okay about it was because she said something first."

"Oh." He sounds disappointed. "What do you mean you ran into her on your way back from school? I tried to pick you up earlier and you weren't there."

"Well that's another thing." I'm just sheepish at the today's events, honestly. "Thompson decided that he wanted to fight in the middle of the school day. He got sent to the principal's office and the principal basically just told me to go home. And I ran into Sadie on the way back."

"Oh holy fuck, Lace." He just laughs nervously. "I wanna ask if you got totally fucking creamed, but I also wanna know why the fuck he did that."

"Well, I didn't get 'creamed' ehh heh. I was winning until the principal turned the corner, and suddenly Thompson was on top of me. He only looked like he was winning when the principal came around. And I don't know why that happened. I was surprised when you said that you were held at gunpoint to take Nail to the tallest building and you said that he wasn't there? I mean, isn't he kinda a big deal in there? Something must've happened."

"Ahaa, fuck yeah, Lace! I still don't know why Thompson wasn't there though."

"Hey, Blue?"

"Yeah?"

"Do you think that I could see you today? I wanna hear about the whole gunpoint thing, but something else kinda happened, and I kinda feel like I need to show you some of it for you to get it," I gingerly pick up the court letter between two of my fingers. "I also have a feeling that I'll need a hug later, ehh heh." I'm so nervous.

"Yeah, okay. Did you want me to come over?"

"Yeah, yeah that sounds good. I'll see you soon, Blue."

Right after we hang up, a thought pops into my head. And it's risky, but it might do something about the whole Nail thing. I start to unpack and repack a couple of things into my bag. I wanna try something. The sun might set soon, so I search around and grab a couple pocketknives from my room. Running into the kitchen I grab a screwdriver that I think might fit, and a second one just in case. I put the letter and Mister's phone number into my bag, too. By the time that I think about downsizing to a bag that's smaller than my backpack, Blue's already knocking on my door.

"I'm coming! Just a sec!" I open the door and see his sweaty, concerned face. "Hey, Blue. Thank you for coming over."

"Hey, Lace. Don't hug me, I'm sweaty." But I lean over and hug him through the door anyway.

"Come on in." I scoot over to the hinge side of the door and let him walk into my house again, as I walk back into the kitchen to the school bag sitting on the table. I take out the letter that I got from the government about my case with Rosalyn. Come to think of it, why did I even put the letter into the bag in the first place? I knew that I was gonna show him anyway. "I need to show you this, but it might make you pretty mad." Gingerly, I hand him the opened envelope.

He only reads the page for half a moment before he reacts. But he doesn't get angry. Instead, he just gets kinda sad looking. "Aw, fuck, Lace. I'm sorry. I'm sorry it didn't go through. Do you know what happened?"

"Mr. Smith called me directly, said that some of the evidence was compromised. Something must've happened with the pictures after the camera got handed off. Without that stuff I guess we didn't have enough evidence."

"Rosalyn must've lied her ass off."

"I thought that too, ehh heh. But, I mean, why wouldn't she? If she confessed about anything that would fuck up her future. Certainly doesn't serve her to be honest about it. Mister said that if I wanted to try and go forward with the case anyway, I could call him, and he'd try to help even though it'd be harder."

"Do you think you're gonna? Do you think you'd even get the chance to try?"

"I don't know. I'm starting to wonder if it's even gonna be worth it. Now it's a case about tampered evidence that might not even prove anything after all. If it doesn't work now, I don't even know if I should bother."

"If I were you, I would try..." He thinks for another moment before he continues. "But I'm not you. I know that it's probably a lot for you to even think about right now."

"Yeah, it really is. I don't know how I've been holding up, honestly. As soon as I talked to Sadie, I just fell apart. If I talked about it in court, I might just fall apart again. It might be just too much. But what if it's time sensitive?"

"It wouldn't surprise me if it was, but we need to worry about Lacey Matthews in the right now. We don't need to worry about the legal system. We need to make sure you're okay before we make sure that Rosalyn gets hers, okay? It's okay if you don't. It's okay if you don't think that you can."

"But I feel like I should, y'know? I feel like it could make a difference or something."

"It'll be a major difference to me if you wind up being not okay in the long run. Stress can do a lot of things to you, Lace. I don't need you winding up like me after Donte died. Not if we can help it."

"Do you think that would happen?"

"I don't know, not for certain. I'll support you whichever you choose, but you'd have to promise me you'd wind up still being yourself when you get to the other side of it."

"I might need to think about it."

He hands the letter back to me.

"I think I should put this in my room for safe keeping. I wouldn't want to lose it, just in case."

He stands back for a moment.

"You can come too, Blue. Maybe it'll be more comfy than just standing in the kitchen." When we're there, I invite him to sit on the edge of my bed. "Tell me what happened with this morning."

"I mean, I don't know what there is to say. Basically a bunch of people were knocking at my door at like five this morning. They claimed that they were from Nail. It was a bunch of guys that I didn't even recognize, and one of the guys had a gun. Some other guy told me that they were gonna take me to the tallest building and that I was gonna show them how to get up there. I did the whole thing with the rope and the weight. I aimed at the hook a couple of times— I think I missed a lot more because I was pretty nervous— but I eventually got the rope up there the right way. I thought I was gonna die up until that point, but things calmed down after that."

"What, so after that, did they let you go?"

"Nah. They told me to get up there to prove that I wasn't lying. I shimmied up the rope up to the second floor. A couple of their guys tried to follow me, but only one of those guys had enough upper-body strength to get up there, I guess. Kinda thought they were gonna shoot me in the back while I was climbing up or something, but I knew that if I didn't climb up, I was gonna get shot anyway."

Somehow, at this point, I've managed to wrap him into an awkward hug. He's shaking a little at the recount. I stroke his hair. He calms down.

"Obviously, I didn't get shot. The guy followed me onto the second floor, and I told him that we climbed up the staircase the rest of the way up because the elevators are busted.

So we went up a bunch of flights of stairs until we got to the top. I could tell that he was pretty winded when we got there, but he looked down over the side. He shouted something down at the rest of the guys that I couldn't totally catch, but my guess is that he was letting them know it was real. He told me that we could head back down."

"How did you get down anyway? Shimmy down the rope again? I think you had me pull up the rope the first time. The police had us take a ladder before."

"If I were nice, we could've had him go down the rope, but I told him it was faster to go out a different second story window and land on an old mattress that was out there. In retrospect, it wasn't smart 'cause he could've gotten hurt, but he landed just fine. It's how the two of us would've gotten out the first time."

His voice kinda catches on the word *would've*. It makes me sad to remember, but I don't say anything about it. "So did they just let you go after that? You just went back home?"

"Yeah. I think they wanted to scare me though. 'Cause they shot off a couple bullets in my direction without actually hitting me, when my back was turned."

"But they were just fireworks?"

"Yeah, just fireworks. I don't even have a scratch." He hugs me extra hard, and I hug him back even harder. I think we both needed it.

"So, what now? I mean, we don't know why Thompson beat me up today. We don't know what the rush job with the building was today. I just don't get it, Blue."

"I don't either, but I have a pretty bad feeling about it. I always thought that Thompson was kinda on our side, y'know? Like, I know he's in Nail, but he seemed like one of the better ones."

"I know what you mean." I wonder if right now is a good time to tell him about what I'm thinking. "Do you think that we could do anything about it?"

"Oh, no, what do you mean?"

"What if we just made it so that no one could get up to the roof of the tallest building?"

"Wow, wow, wait. What if I wanna go back up there?"

"Blue, why do you wanna go back up there?"

He's quiet. He's thinking about wanting to kill himself again, I can tell.

"Blue, I'd rather you not have access to that place anymore. I know that you felt safe there, but we can always talk here. We can go to college next year. We can be safe here. We can be safe at school. We can get an apartment together, maybe, and that can be a safe place."

He's still thinking.

"Hey." I grab his arm to get his attention. "I want you to be alive, okay? I care about you a lot. I fucking love you, and I need you, and everything is gonna be okay."

"I love you too, but how do you know everything is going to be okay?"

"I just do. You're so much better than most of the people we've talked to, for as long as I've lived here, I've thought that about you. If you die and they live, then there's less good people here. There's less people talking about things that actually matter. Shit is gonna hurt less. We're gonna get out of here, and you're gonna hurt less, and we're both gonna hurt less. I promise, okay? I fucking promise. And I would never lie to you."

He just nods quietly. I don't know how receptive he was to that, not until I see a single tear roll down his cheek. He goes in for another hug, and we just sit there for a while.

By the time that he comes around to no longer having access to the rooftop, I tell him what I'm thinking. "I have some screwdrivers. I have some pocketknives. I bet we can try to screw off the hook we've been using. Then no one can get back up there anymore. For all the harm that Nail probably plans on doing with it, I think it might be worth a shot."

"Yeah, okay. Let's go then."

By now the sun has set and it's completely dark outside, except for the moon. I mount his handlebars and we head out to the tallest building again.

When we get there, everything is mad. There are fist fights happening outside, and I think that if it weren't dark, we would've been spotted and chased down. There are pale little people sticking out of a bunch of the higher balconies and throwing things down. Some of them have guns, but, luckily, most of them don't try to shoot. There's too much movement with the fist fights going on outside. Not enough clear shots.

It's clear that most of the fights are happening between people from Nail and Wood almost immediately. One of the fighters is almost always white, another almost always darker in color. Very few Asians are around, might I add. I don't know what everyone here is trying to achieve.

We decide to leave the bike a couple of buildings away where no one could see the reflective tape very well.

"How do we get in there?" Blue asks me, expecting me to know what to do. I guess this was my idea, after all.

"I don't know. I didn't know that this would be happening here already. We'd draw a lot of attention if we tried to climb up the rope now." The plus side of there being a fight around the building right now, is that the rope has already been put up. And it looks like no one is trying to stand guard at the bottom or the top of it. Seems irresponsible, but it definitely works in our favor that way.

After a few minutes of carefully watching the rope from a distance, we notice that people periodically go up the rope. Sometimes, we can tell, it's because they've finished up their fist fight and they want to try out the view from the inside. Maybe they're hoping they can shoot too.

The two of us finally come up with an idea to get over there without being noticed a whole bunch.

"You have to pretend to fight me, and you have to pretend to win. I'll lay low afterwards. It looks like no one is paying any of the losers much mind afterward. And everyone is spending so much time scuffling with each other they wouldn't even notice if we popped up, I don't think. If you go in, you'd have more time. There's no way they'd let me up there. At least you'd have a chance to pass and duck out."

"I hope you're right." I look up nervously at the boys (every once in a while, there's a girl) at the balconies. Their heads are practically glued facing downward. "The people on the balconies probably wouldn't notice us either."

So we hurry over. And when we find a clear enough space, I punch him, hard.

"I said pretend to fight me." He speaks softly through clenched teeth.

"Sorry."

I pretend to punch him in the stomach a couple of times, and he pretends that he's been hit really hard. I maneuver him so his head is in my armpit, between my right arm and my side, and I pretend to elbow him in the face.

He pretends to struggle, but I nearly lose my balance because I'm not prepared for it. To be fair, he probably wasn't prepared to be in my armpit either. And then he grabs my side and actually (ACTUALLY) knocks me over. I can't tell if it was an accident or not. Regardless, I instinctively sit down hard and wind up on top of his abdomen.

For a split second I think that he might've actually gotten hurt, but I have to pretend that I don't care right? Otherwise we'll get caught. But he manages to flash me a thumbs up anyway.

I'm hoping that means that he didn't hit his head first and that he isn't in a lot of pain. Maybe he controlled the fall? I'll have to ask later.

I shimmy up the rope as quickly as I can, backpack still on my back (thank god it's black, so no one can pick me out). Before today, when Thompson fought me, I guess, I'd never fought anyone with any extra cargo before. And now it's happened twice in one day. Granted, when I fought Blue it was staged, and my bag is pretty light. Maybe I'll just count the one fight from earlier today then.

I chuckle to myself at the thought of that, two fights in one day. Before today I certainly hadn't actually fought much before, though my dad and martial arts classes had trained me for some of it, sorta? It's kinda ridiculous that I did that well earlier against Thompson. Who knows? Maybe he's actually pretty weak and there's nothing to be proud of in reality, but I find that a little hard to believe.

When I reach the top of the rope, I mentally prepare myself for not having much time. I go through scenarios of someone coming in after me because they decide that they're done fighting their counterpart from Wood, of someone being on their way out, of someone standing in the corner and having a gun on me. But there's no one here. Everyone must be up higher with their guns, on the balconies and looking down at the fighters. I thought that most of them would be up there, but I didn't think that the entry floor would be totally abandoned.

I launch myself in and check behind me, double checking that no one was climbing up at the same time. All clear.

I take the rope off the hook by nudging the "U" off the cold metal. Everything is pretty loud outside, but when I listen for it, I can hear it land with a soft "pthunk" a floor below. Quickly, I unzip my backpack open and take out the smaller of the two screwdrivers, and it fits perfectly—the way I thought it would—as I unscrew one screw. The second screw.

It's rusted itself into the wall, so I try to jiggle the metal out of place with my bare hands. It only budges slightly. I take out one of the pocketknives—I really should have given Blue the other one before I came up here, just in case things got nasty outside—and work my way around the hook. Now, I look outside the window at where Blue is meant to be laying on the ground where I've left him, but he's no longer there. Fingers crossed he snuck away to safety and he didn't need the knife anyway.

I catch it in my hand. I almost catch it too late 'cause I didn't have my hand out when I was cutting around the edges. I could practically hear it hit the ground in my imagination. Would it have attracted a lot of attention? Would it have just sounded like someone dropping a pocketknife outside? No, it would've been much louder. It would've fallen from much higher up. Good thing I caught it.

I head directly to the room that Blue said would have the open window—233—at the very end of the left corridor hallway. I'm hoping that no one else is in there when I walk in.

I don't think there'd be a reason to because so many people are hyped about the higher stories and watching the fight from below. Everyone should be outside or way upstairs, especially if the space with the rope entrance was cleared.

When I'm right outside the door, I hear pacing. I hear someone muttering under their breath. How much can I hope that it's just a really fucking high Weedo? Can I be sure? Is it worth it to risk it? I mean, what if the person inside has a gun and it isn't Weedo at all? What if it's one of the guys that held Blue at gunpoint this morning?

What's an excuse I could use? Oh, Marshal called my home phone and said that I should come get in on the fun! Oh, he was just so excited that Brigham and I helped Nail get into the building!

Deep breath.

Push the door open.

It isn't Weedo.

It isn't Marshal.

It's actually Thompson. He's by himself. His eyes widen and his mouth opens a little, and he stops pacing for a moment.

"Oh, it's you."

CHAPTER 12

CLOSED

——

"Why're you even here?" He starts pacing again.

"Umm— Marshal— uhh— he—," I suddenly can't talk. The words are caught in my throat.

"Listen, I'm sorry about earlier, okay? I was drunk out of my mind."

What's with this sudden honesty? "Oh, uh, in the middle of the school day?"

"Yeah, is that a problem?"

"I guess not, but why? Is everything oka—"

"Everything's fine! Just shut up about it and get out of here!"

"Thompson, what's going on?"

"I don't wanna talk about it."

"Is it your mom again?" I don't know why I asked that. It just slipped out. I just remember.

"The fuck are you talking about, Matthews?!"

"I know she used to hit you." Why don't I shut up?

"I— That's not what happened today. I don't even know why you think you know that. I'm fine." He's obviously pissed. I don't think at me though. But that doesn't really matter if he's just gonna try to hit me again anyway. Would he? He hadn't before today.

He stretches to put the crooks of his arms over his head, making a rectangle with his shoulders and his head in the center. I might imagine it because the light is so low, but I think I see shadows on the sliver of his stomach.

"I can't make you talk about it, but I'm sorry."

He doesn't respond.

"Why did you hit me today? I mean, I know you were drunk and angry probably, but were you angry at me?"

"Hah, what? God no. What the fuck would a little chink like you even do to piss someone off? Before today, I bet no one thought you could put up a fight."

I cringe when he says the word. "Don't call me that. That's fucked."

"What? Oh sorry." Is he genuinely embarrassed?

"If you weren't pissed at me, what happened?"

"I deal with enough at home," I think of his mom again, "but I overheard that they were gonna take a gun to Mathis' head if he didn't show us the way in today. I thought we were gonna wait."

"Why'd you take it out on me?"

"Fuck, I don't know. I'm sorry, aight? You were the first person I thought of. I'm sorry. I'm fucking sorry, okay? You gotta believe me. You didn't do shit to anyone."

"Okay. I believe you."

"Don't go spreading any shit about me getting beat up by you, okay? I was drunk. That's the only reason you got out clean. And if we didn't get caught I woulda creamed you anyway."

"Sure, whatever you want, Thompson. Maybe we can do it again sometime."

"Aha—" He looks like he can't believe what he's hearing. He almost smiles. "Get outta here." At that exact moment he paces right in front of the window and stops. He's all silhouette now.

"You're in front of the exit down."

"Oh, shit. This way's faster huh? Let me get out of your way."

"See you around, Thompson."

"See ya, Matthews."

I wonder if he'll be mad at me later. Maybe we'll actually fight again and he'll really be pissed at me.

The window in this room is a little higher than I expect it to be. It hits me at the stomach when I wish that I could bend at the waist. But I peak over. The mattress is definitely a king size, and it's only about a foot away from the wall. It seems doable, but also what the fuck was Blue thinking when he did this? And how much is this gonna sting when I get down?

Well, Blue's done this a couple of times, and he's fine. And how tall are these ceilings anyway? I mean, I've never been to the first floor, but it looked like Thompson could reach for the ceiling and actually brush it with his fingertips if he bounced a little. It'll be fine right?

Doesn't matter if it'll be fine. It's the only way down now. Thompson doesn't know that, though. Blue and I are the only ones that do know.

Deep breath. Sit on the ledge, keep my knees bent on the way down, feet first. Push.

When I'm going down, I wonder how much all of this really mattered. Now that people are up here already, are they gonna find some way to get into the building anyway? I land and I start to wonder on some scenarios. Would they make a rope ladder and throw it up to someone who offers to stay inside? Has anyone thought of that before? I guess no one's tried to do it before because, as far as I know, Blue and I were the only ones who'd been up there in years. Maybe they'll think of something, and maybe they won't. But Blue and I tried, right?

Why did we do this? I mean, obviously I don't want Blue to try and jump down again, so that's a plus. But what's the harm in Nail or Wood having access to it? They haven't even made any use of it tonight 'cause so few people are actually firing their guns. Maybe it's just a symbol of power to them all and they think that they've won. They won something because their brute force got them up there first, before Wood ever got the chance.

Do they think that that makes the white kids better than everyone else? It was a black kid who figured it out. It was an Asian kid who beat up one of the white kids at school.

It doesn't really make anyone better, in reality. I guess it's an ego boost to the white kids that already know that they've got some privilege.

Does that give them more power?

Over who?

How long will the effect last?

Will it even matter when they realize that the only way they knew up doesn't even exist for them anymore?

Or will it be enough that they did it for one night?

I ran into Blue back by his bike. He was standing a couple of buildings away, where we'd initially parked it. I guess no one noticed him sneaking away. Or maybe it was normal for a bunch of the kids from Wood to sulk away after they got pummeled. Come to think of it, when Blue and I were watching the fistfighting, were there any kids from Nail lying on the ground? There had to have been a couple of them, at least. There had to have been.

As I walk over, I start to unzip my bag and take out the hook, and I hand it to him. I leave the screws at the bottom of it, with the pocketknives and the screwdrivers.

"Hah, Lace, why'd you keep this?"

"I actually don't know. But do you want it? I think it means a little more to you than it does to me."

"What would it mean to me?"

"I mean, the tallest building was your sanctuary for a while, right? No one else could reach you. You could be out of the house and you could be a person. You could feel things." Maybe I'm silly and I shouldn't have said anything. Was this overly sentimental?

Even though there's no one following us, he shushes me.

"Do you want it or not?"

"Yeah, yeah I guess I'll take it. Thanks, Lace. Thanks for thinking of me."

"I'm glad you won't be able to get up there anymore, even though I know you're kinda sad about it. I feel like I can rest a little easier at night now. I worry about you, y'know?"

"I'm gonna miss it, for sure. But it'll be good that I can't go up there anymore, probably. You can't be tempted by what you can't even reach."

For a moment I worry that he'll try to find another way up there. I have to quiet my thoughts.

"I know you did this 'cause you care about me, Lace. Thank you, even if I'm not totally happy about it. I know that that's my brain being fucked up with me."

There has to be some reason he agreed to this when he knew that he was gonna lose something he wanted to keep. "Why'd you agree to it so fast? Us taking the hook down, I mean."

"Well, I know you'd want the best for me. But I also couldn't help fucking with them a little bit. They held me at gunpoint, y'know? I know they'll be pissed about it, but they won't do anything about it."

"I think you're right. They wouldn't be able to pin it on us."

"Yeah, I mean no one saw us."

"Actually, I ran into Thompson on the way out. He just apologized for coming at me earlier today, and then he said that he did it because he was pissed about them holding you at gunpoint. I don't know for sure, but I think he could be on our side? I really don't know. He seemed so adamant about it."

Blue doesn't look totally convinced, but to be fair, I'm not really either. Still, it's comforting to think about Thompson being on our side over Nail's for at least a little bit. It makes me kinda half-smile. Maybe we're the ones that are winning instead of Nail. Maybe not. But, still, maybe.

There's a pause in the conversation, but then he offers me his handlebars. He drops me off at my house, and we're mostly riding high on the adrenaline of pulling it off until we get there.

Before he leaves, I give him a hug and I tell him that I love him and that I'm really glad that he's alive, that he got away from the building safe tonight.

And he tells me that he loves me too, and that getting away from where everyone was fighting was no big deal because he pretended to be really confused and ashamed. He emphasized the word "pretended" like he was insecure and trying to make sure I knew that he let me win. I mean, I knew that already. I don't think I'd ever be able to actually beat Blue up, and I don't know if I've ever successfully beat him in much of anything since I'd turned his hand blue in elementary school.

I let it go. "I'll see you soon, Blue." And I smile again. I don't know how much good I did for Pennyworth as a whole tonight, but I know that I'm keeping Blue alive for a good while longer this way, and I'm happy for that. I love him a lot. He's my best friend, and I know that things will get better again. I've seen him happy before. I've seen him calm and stable for months on end before.

He'll do it again.

It'll be okay again.

I've just got to let him know that too, that things will all be okay again. I'll talk to him about that soon, in person. I don't know if he'll believe me, but I hope that he does eventually, one day.

EPILOGUE

___

I wish I could say that more had changed after the night that we took the hook away from the tallest building, but it didn't really. As far as I know, everyone in Nail is still holding their chins up extra high because of it. They haven't tried to get back up, so they've only been up there the one time that we stopped them. I don't think word has gotten out yet about them not being able to get up there anymore. I think that everyone in Wood just thinks that they haven't used it much in the last few months.

It's possible that they have their suspicions, but I wouldn't know anything about that kinda discourse.

A few days after Blue and I got the hook down, I talked to my mom about going to community college after high school, and she said that I could. She told me I'd have to help her pay though, and that I'd have to call her all the time. I got a job at the diner where Blue works (I guess he doesn't work there anymore, though) for the rest of the school year and for that summer. Luckily, I only had to pick up a couple of shifts with coworkers that were dicks to me.

Blue and I wound up getting out of Pennyworth, which is most of the reason why I don't have all the information between Nail and Wood.

We share an apartment and everything, and we see Sadie all the time. I think that soon she'll actually move in here with us, since we've been talking about it for so long. She's been saving up enough money to do it. Now I actually work at a different restaurant, a sandwich place across the street from the coffee shop where Sadie works. Blue got a job on the opposite side of town, working as the cashier at some clothing store. Blue's kinda a far walk to get to during lunch hours, but sometimes Sadie and I get lucky and he bikes over to meet us for a quick bite.

At the community college in the town, Blue and I started taking a couple of classes. I never knew the name of the next city over until we got here, when I read Woodland City College on the cover of the admissions pamphlet. *"Welcome to Woodland"* signs ran rampant as soon as I learned the name, like they popped up out of nowhere after I'd tried so hard to find them previously.

I call my mom every day, tell her that I miss her, and I love her. Tell her that I'll try to visit soon but I don't know how hard it'll be to get through the border wall. That's probably why Sadie hasn't decided to live with us yet. Maybe she still wants to check in on Rosalyn and see her mom. I mean, she used to carpool with her mom back and forth between Woodland and Pennyworth, and that wouldn't be a thing for either of them anymore if she moved here.

I started calling Jen more often too. I think that she's a little more open to talking because I'm finally in college. Maybe she thinks that I'm finally grown up enough to understand things. I think it's really lucky that she got to go straight to a university and that she's been out of Pennyworth for so long. 'Cause she's right: I've only just started to understand things, really.

I wonder all the time if I've made the right decision.

I don't get to hang out in Marshal and Weedo's cool backyard anymore, and I don't even get to see them anymore. That was fun for a while.

Some twisted part of my brain is disappointed that I'm never gonna see Rosalyn again. I think I mostly wanna show her that I can move on, be better without her, that kind of thing.

I wound up not wanting to try to reach out for help from the police again. I was too tired to try. But I wish that I wasn't so exhausted because I might've been able to do something good in Pennyworth, if I could've done something, anything, at all. I feel guilty about it a lot. But I know that it would exhaust me to bring everything up again and to have to recount everything. There might not be much of me left if I put the necessary amount of effort into court hearings, in addition to the academics I'm also trying to keep up with now. Blue had to fight me on it a little bit, arguing with me that he would do as much work as he possibly could to help me out, but I think he eventually understood that I couldn't handle almost any of it.

I never got to talk to Thompson about his mom. And the two of us never fought again either. The most I ever communicated with him after the hook got removed was a sort of recurring cold stare whenever he would see me across the hallway at school, and that only lasted a couple of weeks. He gave up. I think he tried to get a rise out of me, and I think that he wasn't able to get himself angry anymore. He has to know that it was Blue and me for sure, but no one ever tried to come after us (with the exception of the cops who'd set off their fireworks by our houses every once in a while, but that was never because of the hook). I guess he never said anything.

Blue's depression hasn't gone away, and he actually tried to kill himself a couple of days after we found an apartment and moved in. I walked in on him in his room when the door was left open a crack. The window was open wide, and he was leaning most of the way out of it. We're on the seventh of like thirteen floors. There was a slightly bloodied knife in the middle of the wood flooring between the doorway and the window. I think that night I pulled him away from the window and held him while he cried. I bandaged up his arms myself. That night was the fourth or fifth time I promised him that everything was going to be okay and that I wanted him alive and that I wasn't going to leave.

It's been a couple of months since then, and he hasn't tried again yet. I think he could be getting better. I know that the therapy is still helping because he says that it does. I don't understand all of what's happening, but I can understand why things wouldn't stay better all the time. I know he's doing his best. Every day or two days or three days he'll let me know if he's feeling shitty, and then we talk for a while. He slips sometimes, but he's doing his best.

He always says that he's grateful for me.

I always tell him that I'm grateful for him.

He always asks why.

I always tell him that it's because he listens, it's because he talks, it's because I know he cares about me more than anyone else.

We always tell each other that we love each other, no matter what, before we go to bed.

More often than not, he plants a kiss on my forehead before we say good night and one of us has to cross the little hallway that separates our bedrooms.

Dedication:

This book is dedicated to my sister, Sarah Lin Kernal. Thank you for supporting me unwaveringly.

ACKNOWLEDGMENTS

———

When I first started working on this novel, I didn't know where it was going to lead me. When I first embarked on this journey, I didn't know how much help I would need to get over every obstacle, to every checkpoint, and through to the finish line. Writing *We Pretend They're Fireworks* has taught me that publishing a book needs a village, and I'm so so grateful for all of the support. Fulfilling this massive dream of mine would not have been possible without you.

Thank you, first and foremost, to my family. Mommy and Papa, you are an incredible place of support and I know where I can land should I ever fall. To my sister, Sarah, thank you for listening and loving me, even when it's hard.

Thank you to Kalani Newman, for being my best friend and for giving me the inspiration I needed to keep going.

Thank you to Megan Huynh, for the amazing title suggestion which has stuck with me for years.

A special thank you, for everyone who has helped me with the entire publishing process. Thank you to Professor Koester for selling me so completely on this journey. Thank you to Brian Bies, for being a fantastic mentor and for believing in me so fully. Thank you to my Developmental Editor, Jennifer Psujek. Thank you to my Marketing Editor, Heather Gomez. Thank you to my cover designer, Bojan Kosic. And thank you to my Copy Editor, Gina Champagne.

And thank you to everyone who: gave me their time for a personal interview, pre-ordered the eBook, paperback, and multiple copies to make publishing possible, helped spread the word about *We Pretend They're Fireworks* to gather momentum, and helped me publish a book of which I can be so proud. I am sincerely grateful for all of your help.

Kalani Newman~

Craig Messner

Chi Ngo

Baldeep Pabla~

Danielle Martinez

Christine Aardema

Cory Lien~*

Quynh Kernal*

Brian Bies*

Christopher Benoit

Alexander Peter

Megan Donaghy

Tiffany Rawls

Katie Wong

Kiana Sophia Torres Arpon

Megan Huynh

Irina Bodea

Jasmine Silva

Sarah Miles

Christian Nguyen

Kristadel Dajay

Patricia Cuarenta

Ben-Zion Weltsch

Jessica Yang

Sophie Toucey

Will Higbie

Thanh Lam

Michael Schaeffer

Bryan Jiang

Joan Li

Vivian Delchamps

Bergen Adair

Drayton Harvey

Chan Lin*

Jesse Ren

Eric Koester

~interviewee

*purchased multiple copies